# DIRECTORY SERVICES

## Technology and Deployment

# X.500

## DIRECTORY SERVICES

### Technology and Deployment

**Sara Radicati, Ph.D.**

## INTERNATIONAL THOMSON COMPUTER PRESS
I(T)P™ An International Thomson Publishing Company

London • Bonn • Boston • Johannesburg • Madrid • Melbourne • Mexico City • New York • Paris
Singapore • Tokyo • Toronto • Albany, NY • Belmont, CA • Cincinnati, OH • Detroit, MI

Copyright © 1994 by International Thomson Computer Press

I(T)P ™  A division of International Thomson Publishing Inc.
The ITP Logo is a trademark under license.

Library of Congress Catalog Card Number 93-45358
ISBN 185032879x

Printed in the United States of America.
For more information, contact:

International Thomson Computer Press
20 Park Plaza, Suite 1001
Boston, MA 02116
USA

International Thomson Publishing GmbH
Königswinterer Strasse 418
53227 Bonn
Germany

International Thomson Publishing Europe
Berkshire House 168-173
High Holborn
London WCIV 7AA
England

International Thomson Publishing Asia
221 Henderson Road #05-10
Henderson Building
Singapore 0315

Thomas Nelson Australia
102 Dodds Street
South Melbourne, 3205
Victoria, Australia

International Thomson Publishing Japan
Hirakawacho Kyowa Building, 3F
2-2-1 Hirakawacho
Chiyoda-ku, 102 Tokyo
Japan

Nelson Canada
1120 Birchmount Road
Scarborough, Ontario
Canada M1K 5G4

International Thomson Editores
Campos Eliseos 385, Piso 7
Col. Polanco
11560 Mexico D.F. Mexico

International Thomson Publishing Southern Africa
Bldg. 19, Constantia Park
239 Old Pretoria Road, P.O. Box 2459
Halfway House, 1685 South Africa

International Thomson Publishing France
1, rue st. Georges
75 009 Paris France

Library of Congress Cataloging in Publication Data
Radicati, Sara.
      X.500 directory services : technology and deployment / Sara Radicati.
        p.  cm.
      Includes bibliographical references and index.
      ISBN 185032879x
      1.  Communications software—Standards.  2. Computer networks—
   Standards.  3. Directories—Standards.  I. Title.  II. Title: X
   five hundred directory services.
TK5105.9.R34  1994

*For Alessandra,*
*who inspired all this and more.  .  .  .*

# Contents

# Introduction

Directory services are one of the most fundamental, yet least understood, components of distributed network environments. Directories are specialized databases designed to hold network configuration information and provide a quick mapping between network names and addresses. What makes directories crucial to the successful implementation of enterprise networks is that only through the use of distributed, replicated directory services is it possible to grant network users full transparent access to all network resources and other users throughout the network.

Directory services have often been an invisible component in network architectures. They typically have been integrated with applications such as e-mail or with the operating systems themselves. The notion of directory services as an independent network application that offers a set of value-added capabilities in its own right and is accessible to a wide range of distributed network applications is a relatively new one. The design of such distributed, replicated directories remains one of the most complex fields of computer science; it stresses to the fullest our understanding of how to build large distributed systems. In order for a directory service to be effective, it must be readily accessible by all network components, provide quick response times, and accurately reflect changes in network configuration as they occur. These goals are often in conflict with one another.

The X.500 standards for directory services represent to date one of the most ambitious attempts to design large-scale distributed directory services. Three things set X.500 apart from other directory or name service designs. First, it is specified to provide a worldwide directory service that can implement a cohesive naming and addressing structure across multiple organizations on a global basis. Second, X.500 was designed to provide network information of value not just to applications, like e-mail, but also directly to network users. Finally, X.500 was intended from the start to meet the real-life business needs of distributed applications by supporting extensive query and searching techniques beyond a simple mapping of network names to addresses.

Directory service technologies are new, and little information is available outside of technical specifications. The intent of this book is to provide a thorough introduction to the topic of directory services and to X.500 in particular. The book is designed to meet the needs of implementors, information technology professionals, and systems engineers involved in the design, procurement, and deployment of X.500 products and technology.

The goal of the text is to provide readers with a quick yet thorough overview of the X.500 technology, while also describing how the technology is evolving to meet the commercial needs of various environments. The book serves as an introduction to the use and deployment of X.500 directory services, as well as a reference text on X.500 directory services, and should provide a good base for understanding future industry developments in this area.

Chapter 1 provides a general overview of the role of directory services. It describes the different types of directory services that have evolved over time to meet the information-sharing needs of different applications ranging from e-mail to authentication and security. It also describes some of the emerging applications of directory services technology, such as the notion of corporate directory services.

Chapter 2 introduces some of the key technical issues, such as naming and addressing, database design, and replication techniques that are common to the design and implementation of all distributed directory services, whether or not they are based on the X.500 standards.

Chapter 3 describes the X.500 network architecture and explains how it relates to the OSI reference model. It also discusses a number of supporting standards that are key to the implementation of X.500 in a native OSI architecture. Chapter 4 introduces the key functional components that make up an X.500 directory service, and describes the overall behavior of a distributed directory service.

Chapter 5 provides a detailed explanation of how information is organized in an X.500 database. Chapter 6 provides practical advice on the design of a directory database. It defines some criteria for naming and organizing data to best model an organization's information sharing needs.

Chapter 7 provides an explanation of the 1988 directory access protocol (DAP). It uses an ASN.1-like notation to show in abbreviated form what arguments and results correspond to each operation. Chapter 8 provides an overview of the distributed operations of the directory. It describes in detail how X.500 supports data partitioning, what information each directory system agent (DSA) must keep in order to locate entries in the distributed directory information base (DIB), and the algorithms that are used to locate entries in a distributed directory. It also describes the 1988 directory system protocol (DSP).

Chapter 9 describes the X.509 authentication framework, which serves as the basis for providing security and authentication in directory services as well as in a number of other distributed services, such as X.400 message handling and network management.

Chapter 10 provides a brief overview of the 1992/93 X.500 Extensions (the final text was published in 1993) in the areas of replication, access controls, and information management. It also examines the issue of migration between 1988 and 1993 X.500, as well as the impact that 1993 is likely to have on the implementation and deployment of X.500 directory services.

Chapter 11 describes the use of X.500 in conjunction with X.400 message handling systems.

Chapter 12 looks at issues dealing with the commercial deployment of X.500 technology, including deployment by public service providers. It provides a brief overview of Quipu/ISODE—one of the most thoroughly tested implementations of X.500. The chapter also discusses the evolution of X.500 technology to non-OSI protocol stacks such as TCP/IP, and the evolution of X.500-like directory services, such as Novell's NetWare 4.0 directory services.

Chapter 13 describes a number of application programming interfaces (APIs) that were designed specifically for use with X.500 and other directory services technologies. Chapter 14 discusses the issue of directory synchronization; that is, the integration and data synchronization among heterogeneous directory services and X.500.

I would like to thank the many people who reviewed and provided useful comments on this book, as well as the many networking professionals who over the years have attended my X.500 tutorials at Interop conferences and whose questions and curiosity have motivated much of what is discussed in this text. A very special thanks goes to Neil Levine, my editor at VNR, without whose constant enthusiasm and gentle prodding this project may never have been completed.

# 1

# The Use of Directory Services

This chapter provides an introduction to directory services. It defines the types of directory services that have evolved to meet the information-sharing needs of various applications, ranging from electronic mail to authentication and security. It also describes some of the emerging applications of directory services technology, such as corporate directory services, which are guiding the development of X.500.

Finally, the chapter provides a quick introduction to some of the key technology concepts underlying all directory services, especially in the area of naming, database structures, information distribution, data replication, and management.

## 1.1 THE ROLE OF DIRECTORIES

Directory services are network databases that map network names to addresses. Directory services have traditionally been an "invisible" component of the networking infrastructure; the functions provided by the directory service were typically available to other applications programs (like e-mail) rather than directly to end-users. However, new applications are emerging that use the information-storage capabilities of directory services to provide a general-purpose database of name and addressing information to both users and applications throughout entire networks.

Directory services:

- translate network names to network addresses,
- provide a single unified naming space for all network entities,
- uniquely and unambiguously identify network resources,

1

- are location-independent of network resources, and
- provide descriptive capabilities (in the form of attribute information) that can be used to further qualify network users and resources.

### 1.1.1 Name Translation

Translating network or resource names to network addresses is the single most important function of directory services. Directory services provide the mapping necessary to *resolve,* or match, a network name to the corresponding network address. Network addresses are used by the underlying communications protocols to actually set up a connection between two communicating entities, such as two work stations, a work station and printer, or a workstation and a file server. However, addresses are generally too complex and unwieldy to be made visible to end-users on the network. In order to make network access practical for both users and applications, it is necessary that network entities can be accessed through user-friendly names.

Figure 1.1 shows a client workstation that relies on the directory service to get the network address it needs in order to establish a network connection with a file server. First, the client software queries the directory service using the name of the file server to which it wishes to connect (step 1). The directory service looks up the name of the file server in its database and returns the actual network address for the file server (step 2). The client workstation can then use that network address to set up a direct connection with the intended file server (step 3).

If the application were e-mail, the client would query the directory using

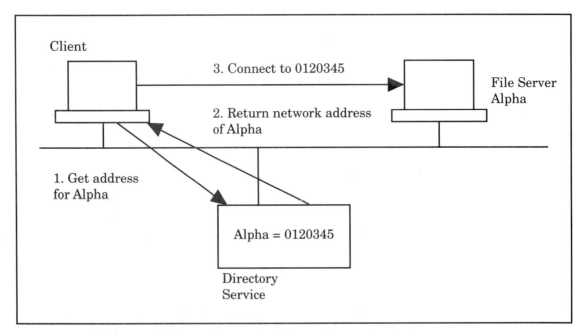

**Figure 1.1** Use of directory in name resolution.

some user-friendly name of the file server (such as MSmith), and would re-trieve the full e-mail address (MSmith@ICL.com) as required by the specific e-mail system.

### 1.1.2 Unique Naming and Location Independence

Directory services also define the *name space*—that is, the naming structure—for the entire network. The naming structure is simply a set of rules that define how all users and resources on the network are named and identified; and en-sures that no two entities are given the same name. Although a particular en-tity may have several nicknames, or *aliases,* it must always have a unique name.

Directory services provide location-independence by maintaining a correspon-dence between network names and addresses: if the network address changes, the name of the resource does not need to change. This is illustrated in Figure 1.2, which shows that if File Server Alpha (Figure 1.1) were to change locations and move to a different subnetwork (perhaps in a different building, thus changing its network address), other users could still communicate with it using the name Alpha.

All that is necessary to make this happen is for the network administrator to change Mike Smith's entry in the directory database to reflect its new network ad-dress (its old address may be reassigned to a different network entity). As long as the directory entry is updated to resolve the name to the new address, the net-

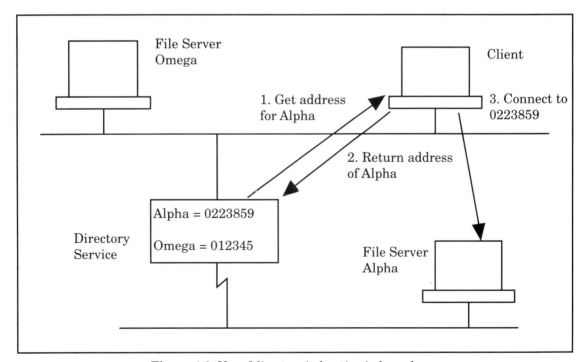

**Figure 1.2** Use of directory in location independence.

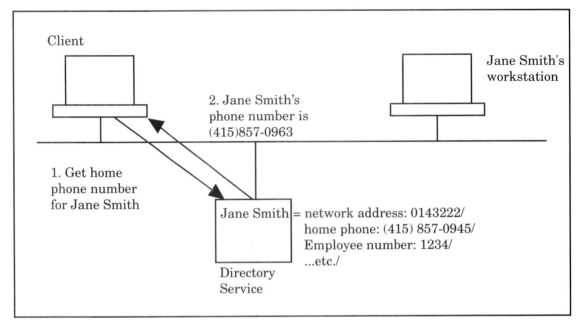

**Figure 1.3** Directory service acting as a corporate database.

work applications and users need not even be aware that the network address has changed.

The directory thus makes it easier to move equipment around and change the physical topology of the network without affecting the logical layout of the network. This is particularly important in large companies, where the average employee moves at least twice a year. Inefficient network and directory design can quickly add to management costs.

### 1.1.3 Extended Attributes

Finally, a newer generation of directories is emerging based on the experiences gained with X.500–style directories, where the directory database can be used to store much more than just names and addresses. It stands to reason that once a database is in place that stores all the names and addresses on a network, the same database can be used to store other pertinent information about the network configuration and resources. In particular, it is desirable to be able to add new pieces of information to directory database entries dynamically, without having to reformat the entire database.

X.500 was specifically designed to support this use of directories by providing a rich structure and set of capabilities for defining new *attributes,* that is, fields in the database record, that store application-specific information about network users and resources. For example, the directory can be used to store a user's e-mail address, fax number, employee ID, salary information, home telephone number, and more (see Figure 1.3).

Information about a user's workstation configuration and available applications (for instance, what spreadsheet programs are installed and running) could also be stored in the directory. The directory thus becomes a powerful utility for all network applications. This allows network management applications to find out the model and configuration of a user's workstation for troubleshooting. Even without talking to the user, a technician could learn critical information such as the type of CPU, amount of memory, the network adapter card configuration, and network software version number on a particular workstation.

In another example, the directory could hold information about the applications a user is running. This information could be used for automatic document translation. For instance, an e-mail application could access the directory database to determine which word processor the recipient of a file uses. The application would then automatically invoke a document translation program to translate the document from the format of the sender's word processor (such as Microsoft Word) into the format of the recipient's word processor (such as WordPerfect).

Directory services are thus rapidly evolving to satisfy the needs of newer applications, which require greater functionality than simple mapping between names and addresses.

## 1.2 AN OVERVIEW OF DIRECTORY IMPLEMENTATIONS

Proprietary directory implementations have evolved over the past decade to serve specific application needs. These implementations can generally be categorized into three general areas:

1. Name services
2. Address books
3. Directory services

Though the distinctions between these implementations are beginning to blur, it is important to look at the key pieces of functionality each provide in terms of how they are implemented today. Name services and address books are currently used by a wide variety of applications; true directory services are newer, provide much greater functionality, and are generally less available. Throughout this book we will use the term *directory services* to refer generically to all three types.

### 1.2.1 Name Services

Many proprietary vendor architectures, as well as public domain architectures such as the Internet, supply name services. The Domain Service (DNS), used in the Internet, Digital Equipment Corporation's Distributed Name Service (DECdns), and Novell's Bindery are just a few examples of name services.

As opposed to true directory services, name services simply provide a mapping between network names and addresses. They typically do not possess the more extensive database capabilities found in enterprisewide directory services such as

X.500. This means their use is limited to a few applications—typically electronic mail, application binding, and user authentication.

There are no standards for name services, since they were developed for proprietary systems. They are, however, optimized to provide high performance for name-to-address mapping.

### 1.2.2 Address Books

Address books are an extension of the mail services in many network messaging systems. Their primary purpose is to provide a quick way for mail users to identify message recipients. Address books are functionally very different from both name services and directory services, in several respects.

- First, address books are often local. That is, they reside on a server in the network and are accessible only to users logged in to that server. They are not common to the entire network.
- Address books deal primarily with the naming information necessary for electronic mail; they do not provide an overall mapping between network names and network addresses, nor are they structured to be a general purpose database. Rather, they only support mapping between mnemonic e-mail user names and the full e-mail address (according to the format required by the particular messaging environment to which they belong).
- The format of the names and addresses that can be stored is usually very limited and rigidly reflects the conventions of the messaging system in which it operates.
- There are no standards for address book architectures. Each vendor has implemented proprietary address books peculiar to their own products.

Address books are currently evolving as vendors seek to transition products into enterprisewide messaging solutions. They are becoming more universally accessible from different parts of the network; that is, vendors are beginning to release products that make shared address books accessible to multiple users at the same time.

Also, address books are becoming more flexible regarding the types of information that can be stored in each user's entry, which again acknowledges the need to include descriptive and addressing information in addition to e-mail addresses such as fax address, phone number, etc. However, since address books follow proprietary designs, they are not easy to integrate across multivendor environments.

### 1.2.3 Directory Services

Directory services are designed to encompass the functionality of name services as well as the functionality of address books. They add more powerful facilities for storing information over and above network or e-mail addresses, and provide sophisticated techniques for searching and retrieving information. The X.500 standards represent perhaps the most complete example of directory service technology available today. X.500 was designed to serve as much more than simply a naming service. Through its sophisticated data modeling techniques and its search and query functions, X.500 represents a major step forward in the design of large distributed directory services. From a customer standpoint, X.500 provides the best opportunity for widescale integration of naming schemes across heterogeneous networks.

## 1.3 EMERGING DIRECTORY APPLICATIONS

Directory services technology is emerging to satisfy two new needs: corporate directory services, and global directory services in support of global e-mail services provided by the public service providers (such as AT&T, MCI, Sprint, etc.).

As these new kinds of services are put in place, they become part of the infrastructure for a new generation of powerful distributed applications and global communications.

### 1.3.1 Corporate Directory Services

Large corporations are interconnecting previously disparate organizations into single cohesive business entities with a common networking infrastructure and a common set of information repositories. This trend is driving the need for a comprehensive directory service that is designed to supply a variety of critical information instantaneously, throughout the organization.

Corporate directory services are information bases that store all kinds of information about an organization's employees and resources. They are a resource for human users as well as for distributed applications. To serve both needs, corporate directories may contain not only communication characteristics but also information from personnel files such as social security numbers, home addresses and telephone numbers, titles, grade levels, salary data, and job history. From an administration and cost standpoint, there is an increasing desire to consolidate this type of data into a single database as well as to rely on automated mechanisms to store and make the information available throughout the entire organization as appropriate.

Likewise, as corporations expand, there is a growing need to develop directory services that are accessible to corporate users worldwide. X.500 directory services satisfy this requirement through the provision of an extensive attribute model.

### 1.3.2 Global Directory Services

Public service providers have a desire to provide a worldwide global directory service in support of worldwide message handling services based on the x.400 international standards. The objective over time is to make e-mail a ubiquitous utility like the telephone service.

Service providers have actively embarked on the standardization of X.400 message handling services precisely with this vision in mind. As they seek to provide a worldwide X.400 e-mail service, they have also found that such a service cannot be usefully deployed without developing alongside it a global directory infrastructure.

While this may sound like a very ambitious goal, it is in effect a major strategic thrust for service providers that view the emerging market for data communications as a new frontier for growth out of the increasingly saturated market for voice products and services. Much of the design of the X.500 standards was heavily influenced by the requirements of service providers and therefore reflects this very ambitious plan. This is evidenced particularly in the multipart naming structure of X.500, which is designed to support thousands of worldwide, interconnected directory services, and the extensive attribute model. We'll discuss both of these in detail later in the book.

# 2

# Key Technology Concepts

This chapter provides an introduction to some of the key technology concepts underlying directory service implementations, especially in the areas of naming, database structures, information distribution, data replication, and management.

## 2.1 NAMING AND ADDRESSING

The main function provided by any kind of directory service is name-to-address translation. Name services particularly have a highly optimized design to support fast read queries. They are so efficient in their name-to-address lookup performance that they actually support the dynamic binding of Remote Protocol Call (RPC) clients and server applications.

The first generation of name service and address book products typically supported two-part (for example, JSmith.WidgetCorp) and three-part (JSmith.Engineering.WidgetCorp) naming schemes. This structure has several advantages:

- It is easier for administrators to manage.
- It is easier for users to remember because the names are short and follow a well-defined syntax.
- It has some performance advantages in that the name space can be searched within a well-bounded number of steps.

However, this structure also has the disadvantage of not scaling well. The experience of most vendors that support a two- or three-part naming hierarchy is that the products do not scale well beyond several hundred directory servers. Also, a two- or three-part naming hierarchy does not always accurately represent the real-life hierarchical levels that need to exist within an organization.

Generally, it is not desirable to link the directory name structure too closely with the layout of an organization (because organizations change often and the name space shouldn't); however, in some very complex administrative situations, a two- or three-part naming hierarchy will not suffice to represent the actual administrative relationships that exist between various portions of the network. For example, if the network is made of many subnetworks managed by different organizations, more than two or three parts may be more efficient (as would be the case with public services).

Most vendors that have implemented a two- or three-part naming hierarchy are now in the process of upgrading that to a multilevel naming hierarchy, for two major reasons: better scaling, and better future compatibility with X.500, which is multilevel.

## 2.2 DATABASE STRUCTURES

One of the critical factors in the design of any directory service is its underlying database. The database is important because it constrains the performance of the system; for instance, a query is serviced only as fast as the underlying database handles searches. It is also important for management and administration reasons. A Standard Query Language database, for example, may not perform very fast queries but may provide some major advantages in terms of standard information retrieval and management capabilities. Generally, designers of directory products face a trade-off: high performance for name-to-address resolution versus extensibility of the database structure and reliance on commercial industry standard databases. The higher performance designs have tended to be based on proprietary binary-tree database designs.

Also, users who are interested in building corporate directories are interestingly looking for products that support user-definable attributes that can be used to store information over and above names and e-mail or network addresses. User-definable attributes can be supported only if the underlying database implementation is flexible enough to support the addition of new fields to existing entries.

## 2.3 DISTRIBUTED DIRECTORIES

Directory services may be either distributed or centralized. In small network environments, directory services are typically centralized, with all the information residing within a single server. This makes database administration very simple, and performance (measured in terms of response times) is adequate as long as the number of users supported is one hundred or less. As networks grow and become geographically distributed, however, it becomes necessary to distribute the directory service as well. This is usually done for two reasons: to improve performance, and to increase the availability of information.

There are several key functions of distributed directory services that should be examined in detail when evaluating directory design:

- Information partitioning and replication,
- Master/shadow and peer-to-peer update mechanisms,
- Caching,
- Synchronization,
- Propagation, and
- Consistency.

### 2.3.1 Information Partitioning and Replication

Distribution does not necessarily imply replication (i.e., making copies of information), although the two terms are often used synonymously. It is possible to distribute directory information by partitioning it and storing different portions of the database on different servers. Typically, some analysis is required to determine the optimal partitioning of information and which portions of the data should be stored on what servers. For example, Figure 2.1 shows a company called Wid-

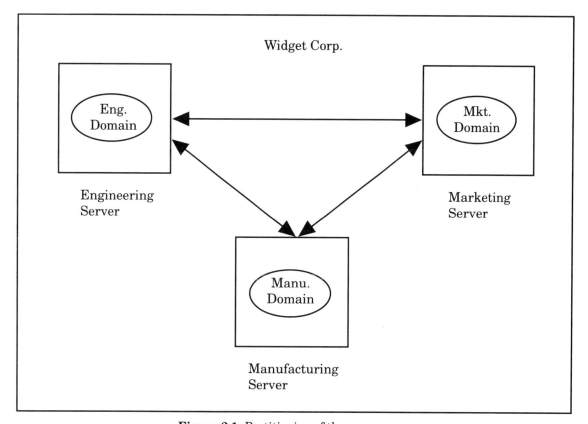

**Figure 2.1** Partitioning of the name space.

get Corp., which is made up of three divisions: marketing, engineering, and man-ufacturing. The network administrators at Widget could choose to partition the company's naming information into three portions (also called *domains*)—one for each division. Each domain would reside on a different server, which would typi-cally be located in the same building and on the same network as the division it supports.

The directory service will need to maintain some mechanism for forwarding data queries among servers. Many techniques exist for doing this, ranging from "trial and error" approaches to rigidly defined algorithmic techniques.

If, for example, the network administrators at Widget Corp. find that the servers containing the marketing and engineering domains are constantly exchanging queries with each other, it may be necessary to go a step further and introduce replication. In order to improve the response time of the queries and overall effi-ciency, Widget could store a copy of the marketing domain on the engineering server and may likewise choose to store a copy of the engineering domain on the marketing server (see Figure 2.2). If it is predominantly the engineering depart-ment that needs frequent access to the marketing domain information and not the other way around, the administrator might have chosen to simply replicate the

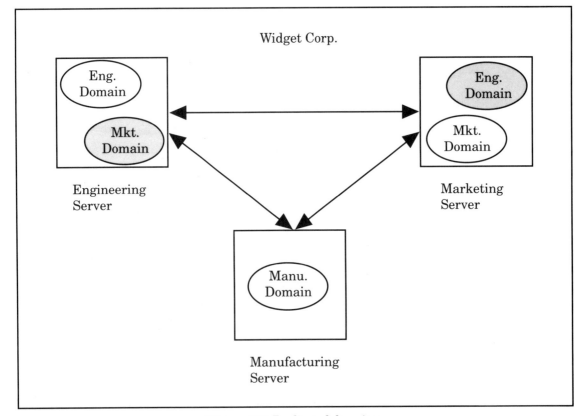

**Figure 2.2** Replicated domains.

marketing domain on the engineering server, but not replicate the engineering domain on the marketing server.

As a rule, replication improves efficiency and performance by placing copies of frequently accessed data closer to the group of users who need it most frequently. However, introducing replication into a distributed system also introduces a new level of complexity. First, the network administrator must decide whether changes to the marketing domain may be directed to either copy or to only the original copy that is stored on the marketing server. Second, the replicated data needs to be maintained up-to-date. Updating can typically be achieved in two ways, master/shadow (also known as master/slave) or peer-to-peer.

### 2.3.2 Master/Shadow and Peer-to-Peer Update Mechanisms

In a master/shadow mechanism, updates are always directed to a single server that holds the *master,* or original, copy of the information. The server holding the master copy is then responsible for updating the *shadow copies,* or replicas, of the information distributed on other servers throughout the network. In our earlier example, the administrators at Widget Corporation would decide that updates to the engineering domain will always be made on the copy of the engineering domain that resides on the engineering server. The engineering server will then update the copy of the engineering domain that resides on the marketing server whenever a change is made.

In a peer-to-peer mechanism, updates may be directed at any replica anywhere in the network. All the servers holding copies of the same data exchange information about which one holds the latest change. At some predetermined interval, all servers update their copies to include the changes with the latest timestamp.

The peer-to-peer approach has the advantage that updating information is easy and updates can be entered into any server around the network. However, it requires much more interaction between the servers to determine which is really the latest version of the information. A master/shadow approach is generally easier to implement and administer, but has the drawback that all changes must be directed to log into the master. This may be more difficult if the master is on another network or is managed by a different part of the organization. Typically, a master/shadow approach also includes mechanisms whereby if the master crashes or becomes unavailable for a time, a new master is automatically selected from the set of shadow copies. Most commercial systems today rely primarily on a master/shadow approach, although some product implementations can be configured to support either mechanism.

Irrespective of whether a peer-to-peer or a master/shadow update mechanism is used, several techniques are available for how the update information is actually exchanged and kept current among servers. The sophistication of the techniques varies by product.

### 2.3.3 Caching

*Caching* is perhaps the simplest replication technique as well as the least reliable. Typically, a server that finds it is always looking up information in a different domain or at another server may choose to keep a copy of the information it receives on such queries. That is, it "caches" a copy of the data it receives. Every once in a while it will query the server in which the information is stored to get a new copy, which may contain more up-to-date information. Caching provides no guarantee that the information is up-to-date. It is only as good as the frequency with which a server refreshes its cache copy of the information. Also, if a change happens to the data immediately after the server has refreshed its cache, there is no way for that server to know about the change until the next refresh period.

### 2.3.4 Synchronization

*Synchronization* refers to the process that keeps different instances of the same information coordinated with each other. Many kinds of algorithms are available for performing synchronization. Some update techniques rely on the use of e-mail store-and-forward protocols, while others require specialized protocols that have been specifically designed to send update information and ensure that it has been correctly received at the receiving end. Essentially, synchronization involves a contract between two directory servers whereby a master ensures that a server maintaining replicated data receives updated copies of information on an agreed-upon schedule.

Some directory products supply synchronization mechanisms within their own environments, but most do not provide synchronization with other vendors' products. Vendors are increasingly beginning to support gateways to provide synchronization to other directories.

### 2.3.5 Propagation

*Propagation* is often synonymous with synchronization. Propagation, however, is when update information is sent out in one direction (typically through the use of e-mail protocols) without requiring any acknowledgment that it has in fact been received and processed by the receiving server. Propagation is typically somewhat less reliable than full synchronization. Most directory products today supply propagation mechanisms.

## 2.4 CONSISTENCY REQUIREMENTS

All commercially available directory services today abide by the principle of *tran sient inconsistency*. Transient inconsistency means that different instances of replicated information need not be updated instantaneously. That is, there may be a lag between the time when a change is applied to one instance of the database and the time when that change appears on all other instances of the same data. This means that there may be a brief time period in which the information contained in the replicas may be out of synch (or inconsistent) with one another. It is assumed, however, that all instances of the information will become consistent at some point (typically within at most twenty-four hours).

Transient inconsistency may not sound like a desirable property of directory services, yet it is essential in allowing different kinds of media to be used to connect directory servers throughout a network. For example, because of the principle of transient inconsistency, it is acceptable to interconnect directory servers via simple dial-up lines, or even satellite links (which exhibit some delays in transmission times). Information may be replicated among hundreds and even thousands of different servers, so it is impractical to expect that a change could be applied instantly to all servers. Even if it could, the traffic it would generate on a network or over wide area links would significantly impact network performance and increase costs.

The converse of transient inconsistency are *transaction-based protocols* (such as IBM's Systems Network Architecture SNA). There are environments and applications (particularly banking) where transaction-based updates would be preferred. Research in this area is still underway and though most directories today do not use transaction-based methods, it is possible that future architectures will support this requirement as well.

## 2.5 ADMINISTRATION

Administration of directory services is probably one of the most complex areas of the technology. Unfortunately, products often concern themselves extensively with the operational design of the system but do not provide adequate tools to manage directory servers. In particular, directory services benefit greatly from the availability of graphical user interface (GUI) tools to set up and manage the database information. Also, administrators need clear and simple-to-follow procedures for adding and removing entries (e.g., information about users or network devices) as well as adding and removing servers from the network. In particular, when adding or removing servers it is impractical for administrators to have to manually update each server on the network to know that there is a new directory server on the network. Directory systems need to have automatic self-registration mechanisms whereby a new directory server automatically registers itself with the other directory servers and becomes reachable from their routing tables.

# 3

# X.500 in the OSI Architecture

This chapter provides a perspective on the development of the X.500 standards. It lists the recommendations that make up the 1988 X.500 standards, describes the X.500 architecture, and explains how it relates to the OSI reference model.

The chapter provides a quick overview of a number of OSI standards related to X.500, including ROSE, ASN.1, and ACSE, that are key to the understanding of X.500.

## 3.1 THE X.500 ARCHITECTURE

X.500 is an application-layer protocol in the OSI architecture, as shown in Figure 3.1.

Figure 3.2 shows how the protocol architecture required to support X.500 relies on ROSE and ACSE, as well as ASN.1 and the presentation layer, as the basic applilcation-layer building blocks.

## 3.2 SUPPORTING STANDARDS

A number of upper-layer OSI standards are key to the understanding of X.500 protocols and technology. These are ACSE, ROSE, and ASN.1.

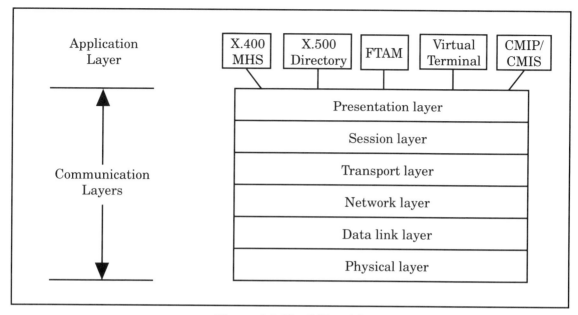

**Figure 3.1** The OSI model.

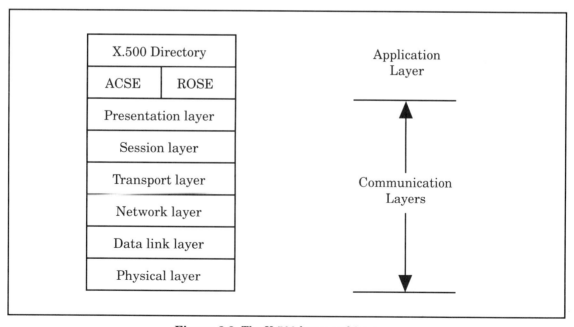

**Figure 3.2** The X.500 layer architecture.

### 3.2.1 The Association Control Service Element (ACSE)

Application-layer associations are logical connections between two application-layer entities that are engaged in carrying out some end-user action. Once an association has been set up using ACSE, it can be used by any number of protocols (such as ROSE) to actually exchange application-level information. In X.500, associations must be established between two directory service agents (DSAs) wishing to communicate; or a directory user agent (DUA) wishing to communicate with a DSA.

ACSE is also used to support the transparent exchange of security credentials, or password information, between two end-systems at the time an association is established. The exchange is considered transparent because ACSE does not enter into the semantics of the security credentials exchanged, but merely transfers them unchanged across the network.

### 3.2.2 The Remote Operation Service Element (ROSE)

ROSE is a request/reply protocol intended for interactive applications. It closely resembles a remote procedure-call protocol in that it may be used to define procedures that can then be executed remotely. It supports four basic kinds of information exchanges, called operation protocol data units (OPDUs):

1. **Invoke** takes an invokeID (a unique operation identifier that is used to distinguish one instance of an operation from another), an operation name, and some arguments. Invoke causes the specified operation to be executed remotely.
2. **ReturnResult** takes an invokeID and a set of results. ReturnResult returns the results of the invoked operation upon its completion.
3. **ReturnError** takes an invokeID, an error name, and an error parameter. ReturnError returns any errors that may arise during the execution of the remote operation.
4. **Reject** takes an invokeID and a problem name. Reject is returned to indicate that the operation has been rejected by the remote system (that is, the remote system refuses to execute the specified operation). Typically this will occur if the remote system does not support the specified operation, or supports an incompatible version of it.

ROSE is used between two application entities residing in the application layer. Upon receiving an Invoke OPDU, a receiving entity may return a ReturnResult, ReturnError, or Reject OPDU. If the operation requested by the Invoke operation completes successfully, the ReturnResult indication is returned; if an error is generated, the ReturnError indication is returned; if the remote application process does not even accept the operation for execution (possibly because of a version mismatch), the Reject indication is returned. Figure 3.3 summarizes the ROSE request-reply interactions that may occur between two application-layer entities.

All X.500 protocol interactions are described as ROSE procedure calls. This re-

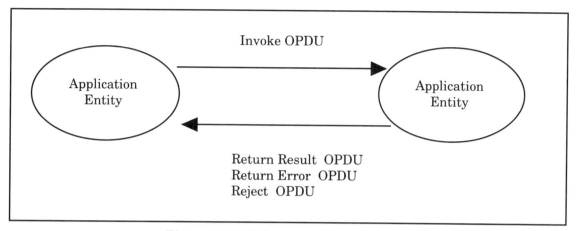

**Figure 3.3** ROSE request-reply interactions

quires a bit of overhead in gaining familiarity with the language but allows for a very compact modeling of protocol interactions. While ROSE was originally specified in conjunction with X.400, it has now been adopted by a number of OSI applications, including X.500, as a useful technique for designing protocols that require a request-reply style of interaction.

### 3.2.3 The Abstract Syntax Notation One (ASN.1)

ASN.1 is designed to overcome the differences in the ways that different computer systems store and transmit information. It provides a common "abstract" language that is used to describe any data structure that may be transferred between two systems. As such, ASN.1 solves the typical computer incompatibility problems such as whether the most significant bit or the least significant bit should be read first.

ASN.1 is the formal syntax definition language that is typically used in conjunction with ROSE. Where ROSE is used to specify interactions between application entities in terms of procedure calls, ASN.1 is used to model the parameters that are exchanged between application entities.

All information exchanged in ASN.1 notation is described in terms of types and values (or set of values). ASN.1 types are formally defined using Backus Naur Form notation (BNF). Identifiers are used to uniquely distinguish one type from another.

#### 3.2.3.1 Primitive Language Constructs

ASN.1 defines a number of built-in primitive language constructs, including:

- **Boolean** is used to represent logical data (TRUE or FALSE).
- **Integer** is used to represent numeric data.
- **Bit string** is used to represent binary data (i.e., sequences of zeros and ones).

- **Octet string** is used to represent textual data or any other type of data that lends itself to representation as a sequence of bytes.
- **Null** is used to represent the null value; it is essentially a placeholder.
- **Sequence** is used to denote an ordered collection of data.
- **Set** is used to denote an unordered collection of data.
- **Tagged** is used to denote data that is semantically tagged for identification.
- **Choice** is used to model data whose type may be chosen from a collection of types that are listed.
- **Any** is used to represent an unrestricted type of data (that is, could represent anything).

### 3.2.3.2 Primitive Syntax Definitions

In addition to the primitive language constructs, ASN.1 provides a set of primitive syntax definitions that can be used to represent any of the above types of information. These include the following:

- **IA5 string** is used to represent textual data conforming to the International Alphabet No. 5 standard.
- **Numeric string** is used to represent the encoding of numeric data into textual form such as can be entered from a telephone handset.
- **Printable string** is used to represent data that can be entered from Telex terminals.
- **T.61 string** is used to represent data that is suitable for processing by Teletex terminals.
- **T.100** represents textual and graphical data for processing by Videotex terminals.
- **Generalized time** models the date and local or UTC (universal time coordinate) time.
- **UTC time** is a more constrained form of generalized time.

The 1988 version of ASN.1 defines a number of additional language constructs and syntaxes not shown above. However, the set described above is typically sufficient to gain a working knowledge of the X.500 protocol specifications.

### 3.2.3.3 Macros

The 1988 version of ASN.1 also provides the concept of macros that can be used to define new, nonstandard types. This allows the above constructs and syntaxes to become the basic building blocks of an endless possibility of definitions. Macros that consist of a series of type and value constructs and any nonterminal definitions that may be recursively built up. An example of a macro definition is as follows:

```
ATTRIBUTE-SYNTAX MACRO ::=
BEGIN
TYPENOTATION       ::= Syntax MatchTypes | empty
VALUENOTATION      ::= value (VALUE OBJECT IDENTIFIER)
```

```
Syntax       ::= type
MatchTypes   ::= "MATCHES FOR" Matches | empty
Matches      ::= Match Matches | Match
Match        ::= "EQUALITY" | "SUBSTRINGS" | "ORDERING"
END
```

### 3.2.3.4 Modules

Modules allow related type, value, and macro definitions to be grouped together. Like macros, they are identified by a reference name. Most of the X.500 protocol definitions are examples of modules. Modules may be imported as a way of bringing definitions from one another. The following is an example of a module:

```
Directory Access Protocol {}
DEFINITIONS ::=
BEGIN
EXPORTS ....
IMPORTS ....
......
END
```

Modules and macros are very similar to modules and macros that already exist in many computer languages such as C and Pascal. They allow for recursive definitions as well as modular approach to the definition of complex interrelated data structures and groupings of definitions.

### 3.2.3.5 An ASN.1 Example

The following example shows how ASN.1 can be used to define a file structure:

```
File ::= SEQUENCE {
    Owner,
    fileName [0] PrintableString,
    createDate [1] UTCTime,
    contents [2] ANY {

Owner ::= SEQUENCE {
    personalName [0] IA5String,
    organizationName [1] IA5String }
```

The above example illustrates a file that is defined to contain an owner name, a file name defined to be of type Printable String, a create date defined to be of type UTCTime, and a contents field that is defined to contain any syntax type. The owner field is then further defined as being composed of a sequence of a personal name of type IA5String and an organization name also of type IA5String.

# 4

# The X.500 Directory Service Model

This chapter describes the key functional components that make up an X.500 network environment. It defines the basic principles of operation that underlie the X.500 design and protocol behavior, as well as the principal modes of interaction available between the various X.500 functional entities.

## 4.1 FUNCTIONAL COMPONENTS OF X.500

X.500 directory systems consist of three principal functional components:

1. The directory information base (DIB),
2. Directory system agents (DSAs), and
3. Directory user agents (DUAs).

The DIB contains the collection of information about users, resources, and the network that is maintained by the directory. The DIB resides physically within and is managed by network servers called DSAs. DSAs provide the actual directory service and implement the service side of the directory operations. DUAs represent the "client" side of the directory service. They represent the user in accessing the information stored in the directory. Users of directory services may be either people or applications, such as an electronic messaging agent acting on behalf of a user.

Figure 4.1 shows the functional components of the directory environment. It shows a Directory Information Base (DIB) being accessed by multiple Directory User Agents (DUAs), either on behalf of users or on behalf of applications, such as an e-mail user agent.

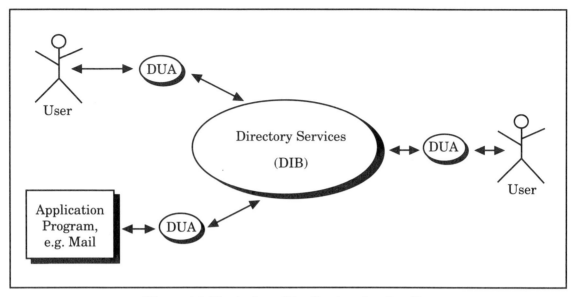

**Figure 4.1** User's view of the directory functionality.

As the information contained in the directory grows, it is usually necessary to partition the DIB among multiple DSAs, called *cooperating DSAs*. This is done to increase availability of the information and improve overall system performance by ensuring that information is maintained close to the network users who need to access it most often. From the perspective of the DUAs, however, such a collection of cooperating DSAs must continue to behave as a single unified database. That is, a directory query addressed to any DSA that is part of the directory service environment must yield the same results as the same query addressed to any other DSA in that same environment. In order to provide this, X.500 directories comprise two distinct protocols:

- A directory access protocol (DAP), which is used by DUAs to access the information stored in DSAs.
- A directory system protocol (DSP), which is used between DSAs to service user queries that require information that might be distributed over multiple DSAs.

Figure 4.2 shows a set of DUAs that access the directory service as a whole by means of the DAP protocol, and a distributed directory service made up of multiple DSAs that interact with one another using the DSP protocol.

### 4.1.1 Principles of Operation

There are three basic principles that guide the overall design philosophy of X.500:

- Quality of service
- Consistency
- Connectivity

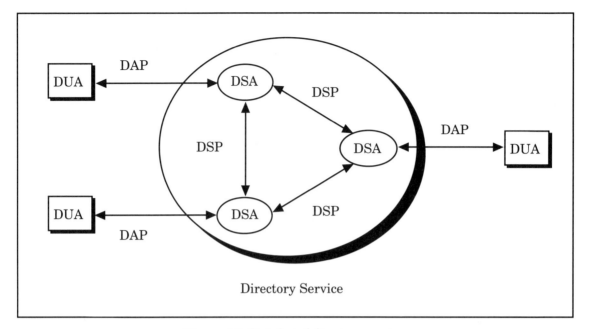

**Figure 4.2** Distributed directory service.

Quality of service refers to the notion that a request (query) may be directed to any DSA in the system of DSAs that make up the directory service. A query must yield the same result (answer), irrespective of where it originated.

The directory is optimized for reading rather than for writing information. This is similar to the design of most name services to date, whose goal is to provide quick responses to queries rather than to support rapid updating of information. When information is updated, the directory is designed to abide by the notion of transient inconsistency, which means that because of updates data may become slightly out of date and there may be a limited time interval in which the same query may actually yield different results.

Finally X.500 is designed to allow a great deal of freedom in what media and types of connections may be employed to interconnect DSAs with one another. Connectivity may include LANs, leased-line wide area connections, dial-up lines, satellite links, and more. Furthermore, the X.500 protocols are designed with the idea that full connectivity among all DSAs at all times cannot be assumed. That means that while there should be at least a single path between all DSAs in the system, it is not necessary for every DSA to have a direct connection to every other DSA. Also, where a connection exists it is understood that this may be a transient connection that is established on a dial-up basis. All the DSA-to-DSA protocol interactions defined by X.500 may operate over diverse types of connectivity approaches, which means that they do not make any assumptions about the connectivity of the network or the amount of time necessary for new information to become available at all sites.

## 4.2 DISTRIBUTED BEHAVIOR

X.500 directories support three modes of interactions between DUAs and DSAs when executing operations. They are chaining, referrals, and multicasting.

### 4.2.1 Chaining

Chaining means that DSAs interact directly with one another through the DSP. Requests for information are forwarded from one DSA to another transparently of the DUA or end-user who originated the query. In this manner, a query may be progressively forwarded by a number of DSAs, creating a "chain" of DSAs involved in responding to the query. Results are collected and evaluated at each DSA in the chain, and are forwarded back through the chain of DSAs to the DUA where the query originated.

Figure 4.3 shows the chaining mode of interaction. It shows a query originating at a DUA being forwarded to an initial DSA (DSA1), which forwards it to DSA2, which in turn forwards it to DSA3. The results collected at DSA3 are then passed back through the chain of DSAs all the way to the originating DUA. Note that at any step in the chain each of the DSAs involved may actually have contributed some results to the execution of the operation. This means that each DSA in the chain will have to collate the results it generates locally with those it receives from forwarded queries. The DUA is handed a complete set of results that includes all the partial results generated at each step in the chain of execution.

That is, if we are looking for the list of all users whose name is "Mary," the query would begin at DSA, and be chained to DSA2 which in turn may chain to DSA3. Each DSA would compile a list of all users it knows about named Mary and return to the calling DSA. DSA1 would collect all the responses and return to the DUA.

### 4.2.2 Referrals

Referrals operate by requiring the DUA to progressively contact each DSA involved in satisfying a query individually. Each contacted DSA returns as many of the results as it is able to evaluate, as well as a *referral,* or pointer, to another DSA that should be contacted to continue the operation. The DUA then proceeds to contact the DSA pointed to in the referral directly, in order to continue executing the

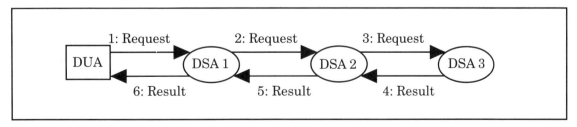

**Figure 4.3** Chaining

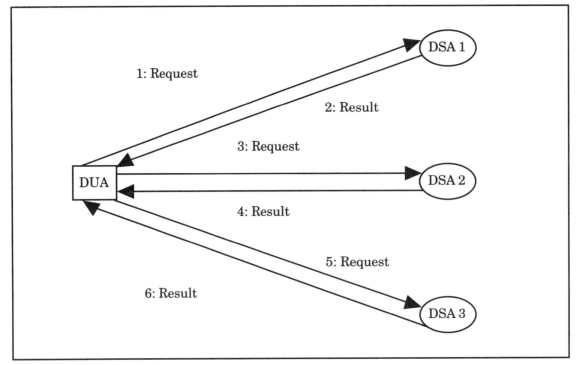

**Figure 4.4** Referrals.

operation. Referrals may be used between DUAs and DSAs, as well as between adjoining DSAs. Figure 4.4 shows the referral style of interaction. It shows a query originating at a DUA being forwarded to an initial DSA (DSA1), which is unable to complete processing of the operation and therefore returns to the DUA any partial results that it may have been able to generate locally, plus a "hint" as to which other DSAs in the network may be able to complete the operation. The DUA then uses the hint, or referral, to contact the next DSA and resume execution of the operation at the newly contacted DSA. Note that in this mode of operation, the DUA is itself responsible for collating the set of partial results it receives from each DSA it has contacted.

### 4.2.3 Multicasting

Multi-casting, as shown in Figure 4.5, is a special case of chaining in that the operation is forwarded to multiple DSAs in parallel. This is not a time-critical operation; it does not have to occur within a specified time period, and does not require that each DSA be contacted simultaneously. It is analogous to broadcasting a query out to multiple-recipient DSAs in the expectation that one or more will be able to satisfy the information request. Only the DSA that is able to continue processing the query will do so, and will return an indication to that effect. Multi-casting is really a special case of chaining where the same exact query is forwarded

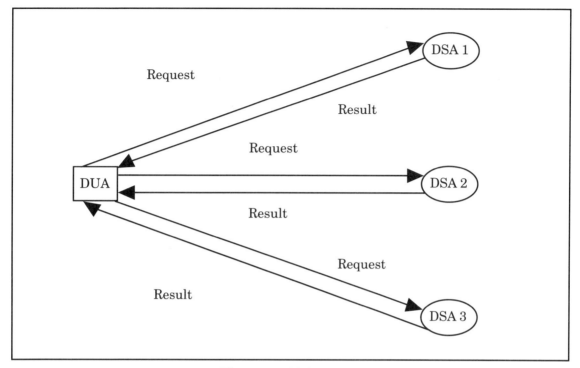

**Figure 4.5** Multicasting.

to a number of DSAs for processing. It differs from the referral method in that the query that is handed to each DSA is identical rather than being a more progressed version of an earlier query. Multi-casting is required only by certain directory operations under specific circumstances, as will be explained more fully in Chapter 7.

### 4.2.4 How Modes of Interaction Are Used

The mode of interaction selected to carry out a directory operation may depend upon user-specified controls set at the time the query is made (more on this in Chapter 6), as well as on a set of administrative policies that may be established by network administrators for each individual DSA. The basic difference between referrals and chaining lies in whether it is simpler for a DSA to forward the request directly to another DSA, or to re-issue the request. Note that generally referrals place a greater processing burden on the DUAs, whereas chaining places a greater processing load on DSAs. The choice of which mode of interaction to use in carrying out an operation may depend on the underlying connectivity scenario as well as on administrative considerations (such as wanting to retain more control over the interaction with the DUA or with the DSAs which make up the directory service environment).

Public service providers had a strong requirement for the chaining style of interaction, as it ensures a single access point into the directory service by DUAs. Private networks tend to be more flexible and often prefer the referral style of interaction, since it allows the DUAs to retain greater control over the execution of the operation.

The X.500 standards specify that DUAs and DSAs may be configured to support any of the three modes of interaction, and that the choice depends largely on local administrative policies. The referral style is the default for both DUAs and DSAs, while chaining is optional. We will see in Chapter 6 that DUAs may request a particular mode of interaction through the DAP protocol. Where the mode requested in an operation is in conflict with that supported by a DSA, the DSA's own preferred mode will take priority. For instance, if an operation requests chaining, but a DSA supports only referrals, the operation will be carried out via referrals. If, on the other hand, an operation requests referrals and the DSA supports both chaining and referrals, the operation will be carried out via referrals.

# 5

# The Information Model

This chapter provides a detailed introduction to how information is organized in an X.500 directory service. It begins by defining how X.500 names work and what principles support the creation of internationally unique names. The chapter gives a detailed explanation of how directory entries are structured and what rules and techniques exist to ensure consistency of information as well as a consistent relationship between directory entries.

## 5.1 THE DIRECTORY INFORMATION TREE (DIT)

The directory service distinguishes between the logical representation and the physical layout of the information it stores. The *logical* representation of the directory database is referred to as the directory information tree (DIT); whereas the *physical* representation of the directory information is called the directory information base (DIB). Each DIB entry corresponds to a vertex of the DIT. Generally, the information stored in a particular DSA is referred to as its DIB.

Figure 5.1 shows a sample DIT, made up of entries for three countries: the United Kingdom, the United States, and Japan. The US name space is further subdivided into an organizational-level name space for a company called Widget Corp. Widget consists of two organizational units, the sales department and the R&D department. Persons as well as department resources are listed under each organizational unit name. Thus, M. Smith is in the R&D department, and A. Jones is in the sales department. In addition, the R&D department owns a printer called LaserPrinter.

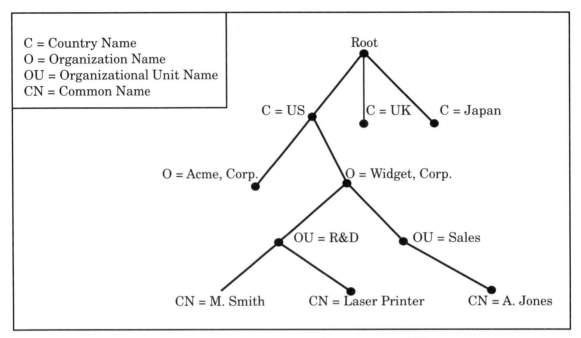

**Figure 5.1** Sample directory information tree (DIT).

Since X.500 is intended to serve as a global directory service, the upper levels of the DIT typically will consist of country entries or entries for international organizations, such as the United Nations. Companies and national organizations are expected to register with a naming and registration authority with each country in which they have offices. This is no different than what is currently done when a company requests telephone service within a particular country, where it is assigned a set of telephone prefixes that fit within the telephone numbering scheme in that country and are also recognized internationally.

In the above example, Widget Corp. has been allocated a name space under the U.S. naming authority. Widget can further divide its name space into subdomains specific to each division inside the company. If Widget were an international corporation with offices throughout the world, each office in each country would register under that country's naming authority. That is, an entry would be created under C = UK for Widget, LTD. (UK), and an entry would be created under C = France for Widget France, etc.

### 5.1.1 Naming and Registration Authorities

Internationally, the directory name space is managed by various naming and registration authorities. Each naming authority has responsibility for one or more branches of the DIT. These authorities may in turn delegate authority for subbranches of the name space to private organizations. Both ISO and CCITT share the vision of a single, unified, worldwide name space that encompasses all OSI en-

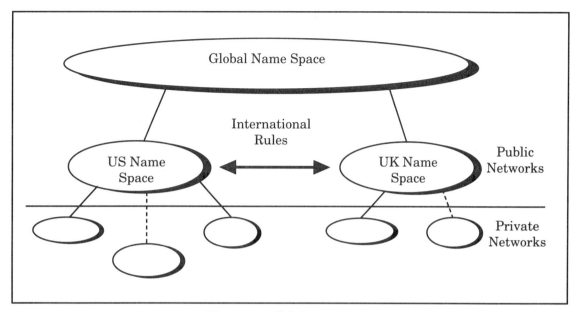

**Figure 5.2** Global name space.

tities, and supports worldwide message handling services. The presence of a unified, common name space is an important prerequisite to the development of integrated electronic messaging services, since it allows all X.400 users and resources to be addressed in the same manner.

Figure 5.2 depicts the notion of the global name space where a global naming authority, most likely ISO and CCITT, agree upon the naming conventions for each country's administrative management domains (ADMDs). National standards organizations in each country, in turn, hand out subsets of the name space to private organizations for use within private networks. This simple process ensures that all OSI services share a common name space, whether they are interconnected or not. Additionally, bilateral agreements may exist at an international level to ensure that naming conventions and message routing are handled smoothly across national boundaries.

The use of a common naming scheme and name space for all OSI resources makes it possible for X.400 entities to address one another on a worldwide basis. The ability for worldwide addressing is independent of whether the various services are physically interconnected with one another or not. It ensures that if a physical path is established between two networks that were previously unconnected, the names and addresses used in the two networks will be able to co-exist and will not need to change.

## 5.2 DIRECTORY ENTRIES

The DIB is composed of directory entries, each of which is typically used to describe a network resource, a user, or a group of users. The information contained in a directory entry is made up of attributes, as shown in Figure 5.3. Each attribute consists of a type and a set of possible values of a pre-assigned syntax. Attributes may be either single valued or multivalued.

For instance, an X.400 distribution list can be stored in the directory by modeling it as an entry where the name of the distribution list corresponds to the name of the entry, and the members of the distribution list are stored as an attribute of the entry. Such an attribute would be an example of a multivalued attribute. For example, the distribution list for the accounting department of Widget, Ltd. would be represented in the directory as an entry called *Accounting,* which contains as attributes the names of the employees in the accounting department. The Accounting entry may contain an attribute that lists the names of the employees in the accounting department (this would be a multivalued attribute) and an attribute that lists the owners of the distribution list, plus any additional information which may be useful in managing the distribution list, such as a timestamp showing when it was last updated (a single-valued attribute).

Figure 5.3 depicts the structure of a typical directory entry. For example, an entry for Country would contain some information about the geographical location of the country, as well as a list of public service providers that operate in that country. Therefore, the entry for the United States might look like:

```
C=US: {location: North America,
       Public Service Providers: ATT, MCI, Sprint, etc.}
```

A company registering under C = US might contain attributes for location, a street address, and the names of the divisions or business units that make up the company. For instance:

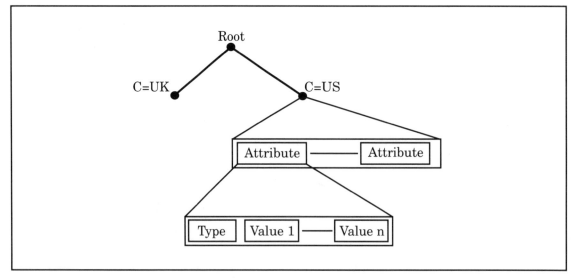

**Figure 5.3** Directory entry structure.

```
C=US, O=Widget, Corp: {
     Location: NY, NYC
     Address: One Financial Center
     Divisions: Sales, Insurance, Travel Services, In
     formation Services, etc.}
```

Finally, the entry for an employee of Widget Ltd. might contain such information as the employee's identification number, e-mail address, business telephone number, home telephone number, birth date, social security number, and so forth.

```
C=US, O=Widget Corp, OU=Sales, CN=M.Smith : {
     Employee number: 983421,
     Email Address: MSmith@Sales. Widget.com
     Business tel: 212-435-7554,
     Home tel: 212-325-7210,
     Birth date: 3-9-1956 }
```

## 5.3 DIRECTORY NAMES

Each directory entry is named by an ordered sequence of naming attributes called relative distinguished names (RDNs). While naming attributes may be multivalued, only a single value is used as the *distinguished value* (RDN) which uniquely names the entry. The sequence of RDNs that lead from the root of the DIT to the object being named, represents the object's *distinguished name*. Distinguished names are unique and unambiguous within the directory, and therefore in the entire network environment. RDNs, which are merely components of the distinguished name, are not unique.

Figure 5.4 shows how a distinguished name is constructed from the concatena-

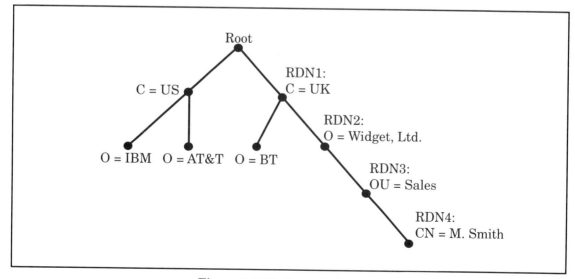

**Figure 5.4** Distinguished names.

tion of attributes beginning at the root of the DIT. The distinguished name for Mike Smith is obtained through the concatenation of RDN 1, RDN 2, RDN 3, RDN 4, as follows:

```
{ C=UK, O=ICL, OU=Sales, CN=Mike Smith }
```

Although X.500 does not specify a particular syntax notation for expressing distinguished names, the notation shown above is typically employed.

If we look back on the example of Widget Ltd. in Figure 5.1, the full distinguished name for each of the leaf nodes can be obtained as follows:

- The distinguished name for M. Smith is made up of the following naming attributes (each of which is a relative distinguished name, or RDN):

```
CountryName = UK
Organization      = Widget Ltd.
OrganizationalUnit = Sales
CommonName = M. Smith
```

Or, using the common notational convention:

```
{C=UK, O=Widget Ltd., OU=Sales, CN=M.Smith}
```

- The distinguished name for A. Jones is:

```
{C=UK, O=Widget Ltd., OU=R&D, CN=A. Jones}
```

- The distinguished name for the printer LaserPrinter is:

```
{C=UK, O=Widget Ltd., OU=R&D, CN=LaserPrinter}
```

The standard does not state specifically how name information should be stored relative to the entries it names. For instance, it does not explicitly mandate that the full distinguished name be stored as attributes in each entry. An implementation alternative would be to store only the last RDN (the one that actually names the entry) with the entry it names and have the directory dynamically reconstruct the full distinguished name through the DIT layout. The standard purposely leaves the choice of representation up to specific implementations.

### 5.3.1 The User View of X.500 Names

The design of X.500 names has come under a great deal of criticism in the industry for several reasons. First, the names are too long. Since the DIT is intended to be a worldwide entity, entries that refer to persons are likely to be many levels down in the naming hierarchy, thus forcing distinguished names to be made up of anywhere between five and ten relative distinguished names. Also, X.500 does not specify a compact notation for distinguished names, but requires that the attribute type be specified in all cases. Unlike other directory specifications, X.500 did not adopt any conventions that take into account the order in which the naming components are specified or that imply the type of each component by its position in the name string.

X.500 was intended to provide the greatest amount of freedom and generality in defining names. The disadvantages of the X.500 approach are also its advantages. The fact that the X.500 structure is multilevel and not bounded by a maximum number of naming components allows it to more efficiently model a truly worldwide DIT made up of potentially millions (or even billions) of entries. The requirement for specifying the attribute type for each name component ensures against errors and guarantees unambiguous identification of entries even in a very large name space where there is a high potential for naming conflicts and overlaps.

Where X.500 does fail, however, is in providing user-friendly names. X.500 names are too long and complex to be considered user-friendly. However, that should not have been a goal of the standard in the first place. User-friendliness can be provided by the user agent (DUA) component in an X.500 implementation. In fact, the naming structure specified in the standard is best understood as the systems' "native" naming structure, which allows the X.500 system to uniquely identify entries in a global name space.

The DUA front-end can provide many kinds of optimizations to provide user-friendly names while transparently mapping these to a full X.500 native name. For instance, in Figure 5.1, users within Widget Corp. should not be required to specify the country component when looking for information within the Widget company name space. Therefore, a DUA front end can be designed to simply identify user A. Jones as:

```
A.Jones@R&D,  or  Jones.R&D
```

when the query is within Widget Corp. The DUA implementation would map this transparently to:

```
{O=Widget Corp., OU=R&D, CN=A. Jones}
```

before handing the query off to a DSA. As long as the DSAs that contain information about Widget are not connected into a worldwide DIT, the country component doesn't need to be used at all. Assuming, however, that Widget is a multinational corporation with offices in the United States as well as the United Kingdom, U.S.-based employees might have to address queries to A. Jones as:

```
A.Jones@R&D. UK
```

The DUA would map this into the full X.500 name:

```
{C=UK, O=Widget Ltd., OU=R&D, CN=A. Jones}
```

In effect, this example shows that users should not need to specify more components of the name than those that are strictly required to identify the name within a particular name space. A well-designed DUA should prompt users to provide additional name components only on queries that go outside the normal name space.

### 5.3.2 Alias Names

Directory entries may also possess alternative names, called *aliase*. Aliases provide alternate names for entries as well as a shorthand way of referring to entries. Figure 5.5 illustrates the use of aliasing. User M. Smith in the DIT can be accessed either through his full distinguished name {O = Widget UK, OU = Sales, OU = Administrators, CN = M.Smith} or through an alias name {O = Widget UK, CN = UKNetAdmin} set up to reflect M. Smith's job function. Alias names are set up by network administrators just like any other kind of entry. Users throughout the network can more easily exchange information with the network administrator for the U.K. network than by remembering that M. Smith is the U.K. network administrator.

While the use of aliases provides a mnemonic, shorthand way of referring to entries, it does force more processing on the directory service. In the above example, all queries directed to {O = Widget UK, CN = UKNetAdmin} will require the directory to first locate the entry named {O = Widget UK, CN = UKNetAdmin}. The directory service will recognize that the entry represents an alias pointer (from its object class; more about this later) and will extract from the alias entry the full distinguished name of the entry it points to, in this case {O = Widget, UK, OU =

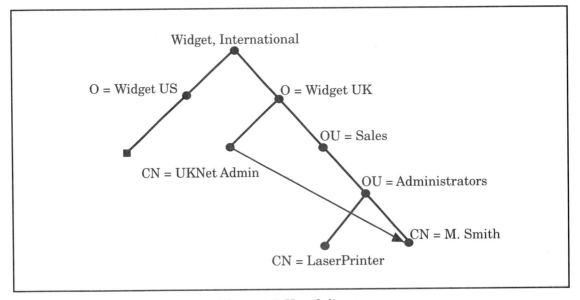

**Figure 5.5** Use of aliases.

Sales, OU = Administrators, CN = M.Smith}. The directory must then start the search again in order to locate the actual entry for M. Smith.

## 5.4 ATTRIBUTES

Each directory entry is made up of attributes that provide specific information about particular characteristics of a network entity. An *attribute* consists of a type and a set of possible values of a specified syntax. The *type* is a unique object identifier that equates to an integer value; a *value* is anything within a specified syntax, as follows:

```
Attribute ::= < Type, SET OF Values >
 Type ::= an Object Identifier (i.e. an integer value)
 Value ::= anything within a specified syntax.
```

For instance, an attribute definition for Telephone Number would consist of an object identifier number, such as the integer 15, and a value of syntax numeric string.

```
Telephone Number :=(ID=15, Value=Numeric String)
```

Using this definition, the actual representation of telephone number attributes within an entry therefore would look like the tuple:

```
<15, 212-345-0091>
```

where the object identifier 15 identifies the type of the attribute, and the phone number 212-345-0091 is the actual value.

X.500 allows new attributes to be defined through the use of the Attribute macro:

```
ATTRIBUTE MACRO ::=
        WITH ATTRIBUTE-SYNTAX some syntax,
        SINGLE VALUE optional,
        ::= { attributeType some integer }
```

The Attribute macro specifies that a new attribute type can be created by defining its intended syntax, and specifying whether it will be a single-valued attribute or whether multiple values may be present. As was the case for new object classes, new attribute types are also identified through the assignment of a unique object identifier. An example of an attribute specific to X.400 implementations is mhs-or-addresses, which is used to store X.400 Originator/Recipient (O/R) Addresses. It is defined in accordance with the Attribute macro as:

```
mhs-or-addresses ATTRIBUTE
        WITH ATTRIBUTE-SYNTAX mhs-or-address-syntax
        MULTI-VALUE
        :: = id-at-mhs-or-addresses
```

In the above, mhs-or-addresses is defined to be an attribute of syntax mhs-or-address, which is a multivalued attribute (that is, multiple values may be present for the attribute type). The mhs-or-address attribute type is uniquely identified by assigning to it an integer object identifier called id-at-mhs-or-addresses, the X.400 standards assign an integer value to represent the constant id-at-mhs-or-addresses.

Attribute types may be:

1. Internationally standardized, as are those defined in X.520,
2. Assigned locally by national or private organizations, or
3. Specific to a particular product or implementation.

## 5.5 OBJECT CLASSES

Every directory entry is considered to belong to at least one object class. An entry's object class restricts the types of attributes that may be present in the entry. One object class may be a subclass of another. An entry's object class restricts the types of attributes that may be present in the entry.

X.500 provides an Object Class macro for defining new object classes. Defining a new object class involves assigning a unique object identifier for the class, indicating whether it is a subclass of another class, and listing any mandatory or optional attribute types for the class. The object class TOP is defined to be the superclass for all directory object classes.

```
OBJECT-CLASS MACRO ::=
     { SUBCLASS OF some class,
       MUST CONTAIN some attribute,
       MAY CONTAIN some attribute }
     :: = { objectClass some integer }
```

The Object Class macro specifies that a new object class is defined by stating what other object class it is a subclass of (the default being the superclass Top), what mandatory attributes it must contain, and what optional attributes it may contain. The new object class is identified by assigning it a unique object identifier.

For instance, X.400 users are defined as belonging to the class mhs-user, as follows:

```
mhs-user OBJECT-CLASS
     SUBCLASS OF Top
     MUST CONTAIN { mhs-or-addresses }
     MAY CONTAIN {
          mhs-deliverable-content-length,
          mhs-deliverable-content-types,
          mhs-deliverable-eits,
          mhs-message-store,
          mhs-preferred-delivery-methods }
     ::= id-oc-mhs-user
```

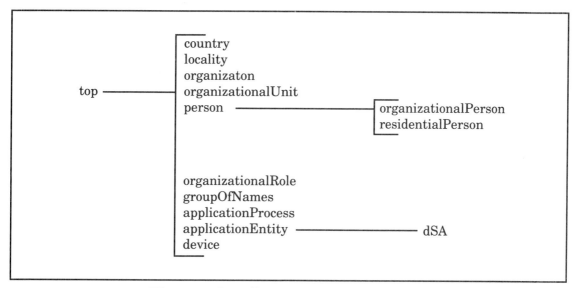

**Figure 5.6** Dependency of directory object classes.

The object class mhs-user is defined to be a subclass of Top, which must contain the user's MHS O/R address (mhs-or-address). In addition, an object of type mhs-user may contain attributes specifying the maximum content length of messages that the user is willing to accept (mhs-deliverable-content-length), the preferred content types the user is willing to receive (mhs-deliverable-content-types), and so forth.

The X.500 documents define a set of standard object classes for use by all OSI applications. Figure 5.6 lists the set of directory object classes and their relationship as defined in X.521.

Note that this is only a suggested set of object class dependencies, and that particular implementations or user profiles may choose to adopt their own structure. Most OSI applications will define a set of object classes specific to their own needs in addition to those defined by the directory standards documents. For instance, 1988 X.400 defines a set of object classes that can be used to model objects and resources in an X.400 message handling environment, as shown in Figure 5.7.

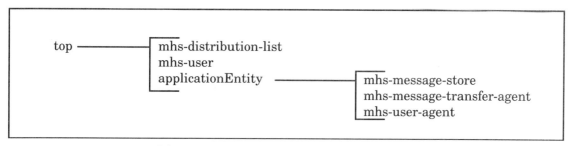

**Figure 5.7** Dependency of X.400 object classes.

## 5.6 SCHEMA

If we consider the notion of object classes, attribute types, and the other information structure concepts discussed thus far, we find that the directory information is made up of a strongly typed set of objects. In fact, the relationship between attribute types, syntaxes, object classes, and entries is tightly regulated. The term *schema* in X.500 refers to the set of rules that govern the structure of the DIT and that define the set of permitted superior or subordinate object classes for each entry. In particular, schema rules define whether an entry of one object class may be placed underneath an entry of another class. This allows schema rules to be put in place to ensure that entries for countries, such as C = US, cannot be placed underneath entries for users, e.g. CN = John Smith.

Figure 5.8 summarizes the relationship between schema, attributes, object classes, and entries. The definition of schema rules generally comprises:

- DIT structure rules, which define relationships between entries.
- Naming rules for each object class, which specify the attribute(s) used in the RDN for objects of that class.
- Object class definitions, which apply to individual entries.
- Attribute type definitions, which apply to attributes within an entry.
- Attribute syntax definitions, which apply to the values within specified attribute types.

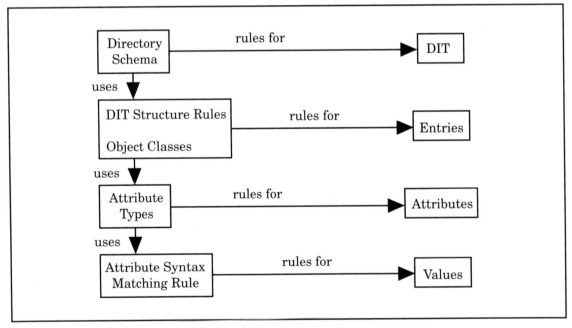

**Figure 5.8** Schema rules.

The 1988 version of the X.500 standard provides no mechanisms to formally define schema rules. The standard merely states that schema rules exist and that the directory service enforces these rules when adding or removing entries or attribute information. The standard does not define a means for determining which schema rule applies to a given entry in the DIT; the result of this deficiency is that each DSA has one schema that applies to all the entries in that DSA. Thus, in effect, in the 1988 version of the standard, the permitted superior/subordinate relationships between objects in the directory are defined via static documentation maintained offline from the directory (typically in paper form). This means that DIT designers and network administrators must agree offline as to how they will structure the information in the directory, as well as which superior/subordinate relationships are valid. This information is then manually configured into the directory implementation so that it can enforce the agreed-upon conventions.

# 6

# Implementing the DIT

Chapters 4 and 5 describe the mechanisms defined by the standards for organizing directory information, as well as for DSA-to-DSA interactions. Chapter 4 provides an overview of how the distributed directory works, and how operations are carried out in a distributed directory service environment. Chapter 5 describes how data is organized in the directory information base, and what rules exist for defining names, attributes, and object classes. This chapter takes a step back from the rules defined by the standards and looks at how these can best be applied to set up a working X.500 directory system. It provides some insight and guidance into how to design an organization's DIT structure and covers issues to consider when implementing a system. Some examples are provided to show how information can be arranged in a typical multinational organization. Nevertheless, the reader should understand that setting up and configuring a directory service requires some specialized analysis and planning that is specific to each organization's own information-sharing and modeling needs.

## 6.1 CHOOSING AN ENTERPRISE NAMING STRUCTURE

The rules for structuring names and defining attributes and object classes as defined by the standard and described in Chapter 5 are intentionally generic. As an international standard, X.500 is intended to be applied in diverse kinds of communications environments, ranging from public service directories to small and large private networks within a particular company or division. Thus, there is no single "right" way to structure the DIT within a company or an organization. The intent of the standard is to allow as flexible a set of configurations as possible to best meet the specific information modeling needs of particular industries and communities of users.

Though the standard does define the set of basic mechanisms for organizing information, it is up to managers and network administrators in each particular environment to decide what information will be stored in the directory and how it will be organized. This is exactly what is done when deploying a commercial database. The database provider typically defines a set of rules and guidelines for structuring data and provides the tools for managing and viewing the data. Each implementation of the database may then adopt a different way to model its data so as to best meet the information-sharing needs of the applications that rely on it. Similarly, the design of an X.500 information base is also application-dependent in that the information stored in the directory is usually organized in such a way as to reflect the needs of the applications that are using the data. Therefore there are no strict rules or even hard recommendations in X.500 on such issues as how long names should be, how they should be arranged, and what object classes should be defined. Each implementation is different and reflects the information-sharing needs of the network in which it is used.

### 6.1.1 Designing the DIT Layout

Chapter 5 discusses the notion of object classes and how directory entries are typed so to belong to a particular class. Recommendation X.521 also defines a set of attribute types and object classes that are intended to be used for naming purposes. Figure 6.1 summarizes the kinds of entities that can be modelled according to recommendation X.521. The diagram describes the recommended relationships among entities and shows in parentheses the naming attribute that is most commonly used to represent an instance of that class. A number of object classes such as organizational person, organizational role, device, and so on use the same attribute type Common Name (CN) to name the entry.

According to the diagram, names can be structured in a number of different ways. Two kinds of entities may be placed underneath country: the name of a locality or the name of an organization. A locality may in turn have under it the name of a person, a group of names, the name of an organization, or an organizational unit name. An organization, on the other hand, can have under it the name of a locality, an application process, a device, an organizational unit, a person in an organization or person's title.

When setting up a naming structure within an organization, therefore, any one of the combinations shown in Figure 6.2 would be valid.

Nevertheless, although all the structures and resulting names shown in Figure 6.2 are valid, the one most commonly used is the one that was presented in Chapter 5, which lists Country (C), then Organization (O), followed by any number of Organizational Unit (OU) names, followed by Common Names (CN).

Note also that individuals may have two names: one to reflect their business identity, and another to reflect their personal identity. It is envisioned that in the not-too-distant future when public service providers roll-out commercial X.500 services,

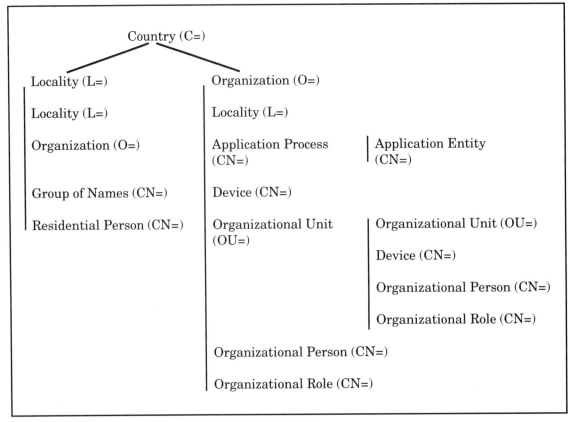

**Figure 6.1** X.521 Recommended naming structure.

it will be common for individuals to register for service under their private identity as a residential person, while also being registered with a different service provider.

### 6.1.2 Pragmatic Considerations

A naming structure within an organization usually needs to cater to several conflicting needs. On the one hand, we want names that are short and easy to remember (typically made up of two to three RDNs). On the other hand, we want to closely reflect the structure of the organization by placing individuals in the correct department and division. The challenge is that most organizational structures are complex, and if we model everyone's entry to match the organizational hierarchy, we will typically end up with names that are anywhere from five to fifteen RDNs (or more) long. There is also a very real danger that our complex hierarchical naming structure will become obsolete very quickly because of organizational changes that occur to meet evolving business objectives. X.500's naming structure can be deceptive in this respect, because by defining attributes for organization and organizational units, it seems to imply that names should be chosen to reflect the real-life

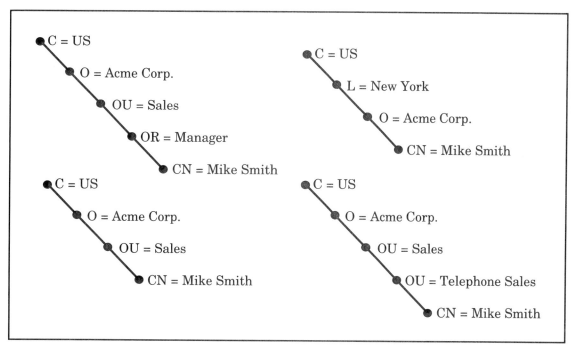

**Figure 6.2** Possible DIT structures.

organizational structure of an enterprise. However, if they were, we would constantly be changing everyone's name to reflect organizational changes. This is cumbersome for the users and can also be a problem because X.500 is not designed to support constant changes to the DIT layout. As we will see in Chapter 7, the directory is primarily optimized for reading information rather than for supporting constant changes to information. Worse yet, applications that are designed to assume a particular name and data structure would have to be upgraded to understand the new information structure.

A better way to set up names in X.500 is to rely on a geographical layout of the network and organization. In general, an individual will move to a new office much less frequently than he or she changes positions, similarly, network equipment (printers, routers, and other kinds of physical devices) rarely move. Therefore, it makes sense to assign names that reflect the location of the user and/or physical resource rather than the actual organizational relationship. For instance, if user Mike Smith works in the Motor Design group Widget Corp's automobile division at the company's R&D facility in Austin, Texas, naming him by his organizational role would yield the following distinguished name:

```
{C=US, O=Widget Corp., OU=Automobile Division, OU=R&D,
OU=MotorDesignGroup, CN=Mike Smith}
```

Whereas naming Mike Smith by his geographical location would instead yield:

```
{C=US, O=Widget Corp., OU=AustinR&D, CN=Mike Smith}
```

Notice that geographical naming typically results in shorter names (that is, fewer RDNs). In the next section we will look at an example of how an organization may be set up according to geographical names.

### 6.1.3 An Example

Acme Corp. has three divisions, financial services (FS), travel services (TS), and insurance services (IS). Each division in turn is made up of the following departments: sales (S), human resources (HR), and professional staff (P). The three divisions operate fairly independently of one another except that they occasionally share management and business information. There are two thousand employees in four cities: New York, Los Angeles, Tokyo, and London. The financial and insurance services divisions are located at corporate headquarters in New York, while the travel services divisions is in Los Angeles. Figure 6.3 shows Acme's DIT strictly on an organizational basis.

According to this DIT structure, the distinguished name for user Mike Smith, who works in the sales group of the financial services division, would be:

```
{O=Acme Corp., OU=FS, OU=S, CN=MSmith}
```

However, by taking advantage of Acme's fairly simple geographical distribution, we could arrange the DIT structure by location as shown in Figure 6.4, thus simplifying the DIT structure considerably. Since the financial services and insurance services divisions are both in New York, they can be grouped under OU = Head-

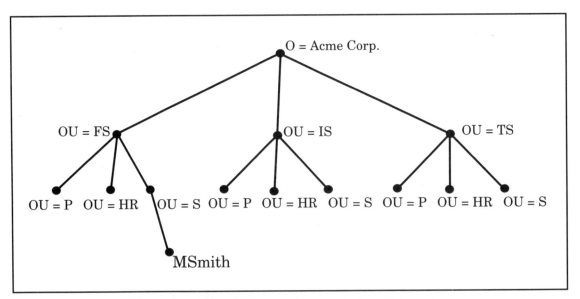

**Figure 6.3** Acme's DIT set up by organizational hierarchy.

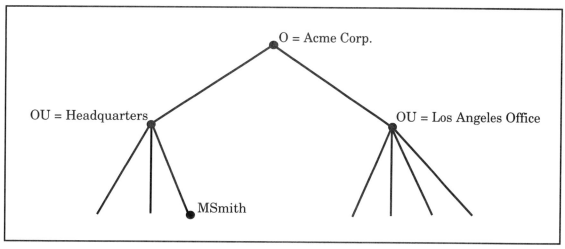

**Figure 6.4** Acme's DIT set up by geographical layout.

quarters. The Los Angeles office, being a disjoint location, would be represented as OU = Los Angeles Office.

Using this new layout, only three RDNs are needed to represent users; therefore the distinguished name for Mike Smith would be:

```
{O=Acme Corp., OU=Headquarters, CN=MSmith}
```

Since Headquarters in New York is a location and not really an organizational unit, we could also have used the attribute Locality (L) defined in recommendation X.521, as shown in Figure 6.5.

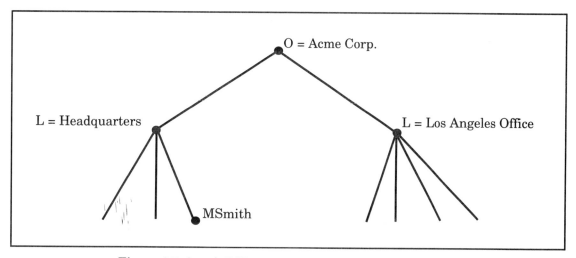

**Figure 6.5** Acme's DIT structure using the Locality object class.

Mike Smith's distinguished name therefore would be:

```
{O=Acme Corp., L=Headquarters, CN=MSmith}
```

While this is correct according to recommendation X.521, it is not ideal, since for consistency's sake most implementations are using the OU attribute type to denote geographical locations as well as actual organizational entities. The DIT structure represented in Figure 6.4 would therefore be the most effective way to represent Acme's structure. Locality can be placed below or above either Organization or Organizational Unit. We could also use Locality recursively to denote various geographical entities subordinate to one another. So, for instance, if Mike Smith were located in Building 1 at headquarters, we could structure his distinguished names as:

```
{O=Acme Corp., L=Headquarters, L=Bldg.1, CN=Mike Smith}
```

### 6.1.4 How Long Should Names Be?

There are no particular rules in X.500 as to the length of names. Performance of an X.500 system is driven by many factors that are independent of how long names are. Long names (containing many RDNs)are typically difficult for users to remember and are input correctly, but they do not necessarily lead to slower response times by an X.500 server. Many other factors drive performance, such as line speed, traffic on the network, CPU power, number of active connections, how the software itself is designed and implemented internally, and more. Flat naming structures are actually worse because by increasing the number of possibilities at every level, the server implementation must spend more time checking for possible matches at every level. The worst possible arrangement for a DIT structure is a flat name space, where, for instance, all the users and entities within Acme Corp. are registered directly at the corporate level under the entry for Acme Corp. This would mean that every time a user looks for a name within Acme, the directory service will have to search the entire Acme name space for a match. In mathematical terms, this search will potentially encompass $N-1$ entries. If we subdivide Acme into two branches—Acme A (x number of entries) and Acme B (y number of entries)—where $x + y = N-1$, then our search space will be reduced to $x = (N-y)-1$.

Most non-X.500 directory services and name services today operate with a two- or three-part naming structure. Often this becomes inadequate in large networks with thousands of users. X.500 names should therefore be expected to be at least three RDNs long. Also, since X.500 was designed to provide a more flexible naming structure that could model real-life organizational issues, it can be expected that in general, X.500 user names will vary from four to as many as eight RDNs. Users setting up X.500 directories should not be afraid to define names with as many as eight RDNs, provided the front-end DUA software is able to provide some optimization in terms of automatic expansion of partially specified names (that is, asking users to input an eight-part name every time they perform directory queries would not be very popular).

### 6.1.5 Using Aliases

Aliases can be used to provide additional names for users or network resources. By defining alias names, an administrator can provide several alternative ways to identify a particular network entity. A note of caution about X.500 aliases, however: there are no alias backpointers in X.500. That is, while the alias points to an entry, there are no pointers from the entry back to all the aliases that refer to it. This means that deleting an entry can potentially lead to *dangling* alias references, or aliases that point to a nonexistent entry. It is important, therefore, to ensure that when an entry is removed, all the aliases that point to it are removed as well. There are several ways to do this.

The automated way is to store as attributes of the entry a list of all the alias names that have been set up to refer to that entry. When the entry needs to be deleted, we can simply read the list of aliases from the entry and delete them with the entry before considering the delete procedure complete. Every time a new alias is defined for an entry, it needs to be added to the list of aliases that is stored as an attribute of that entry.

The alternative approach is to simply keep an offline record of the alias names that have been set up for an entry. The process is the same as that described above: an administrator would delete the entry and then delete all the alias entries that have been recorded for that entry. When setting up a new alias, care should be taken to also record the name of the alias. The alias information recorded offline should be made available to all network sites that might need it by regularly publishing an up-to-date register of the alias-name information.

### 6.1.6 Relating the DIT Structure to X.400 O/R Addresses

A mistake commonly made when first attempting to integrate X.500 names with X.400 O/R addresses is to believe that there is (or should be) a direct mapping between the two. This misconception occurs because the two forms of names look deceptively similar in that they share a number of common naming attributes. For instance, Mike J. Smith's O/R address might be:

```
C=US, ADMD=SpeedyNetService, PRMD=AcmeNet, O=Sales,
G=Mike, I=J, S=Smith
```

According to X.400 naming structure, C denotes country, ADMD is the service provider network, PRMD is the name of the private network to which Smith's mailbox is attached, O is the name of the organization he works in, G is his given name, I is his initial, and S is his surname.

Mike J. Smith's X.500 name, on the other hand, would most likely be;

```
C=US, O=Acme, OU=Sales, CN=Mike J. Smith
```

Where C is country, O is the organization Mike works for, OU is the organizational unit, and CN is the common name.

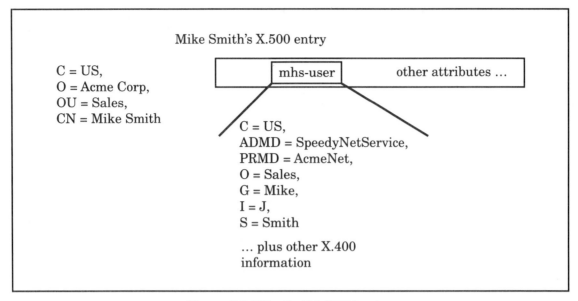

**Figure 6.6** Mike Smith's X.500 entry.

Though these two structures share some resemblance, there is no good way to transform Mike's O/R address into his X.500 name or vice versa. Rather, Mike's O/R address should be stored in the directory as part of his directory entry. When sending mail to Mike Smith, we would then first query the directory, passing in Mike's X.500 name. We would find the entry for Mike and read out of it the attribute mhs-user (Figure 6.6), which contains Mike's O/R address. X.400 has specifically defined the attribute type mhs-user (shown in Chapter 5) for this purpose—to contain the O/R address as well as number of other pieces of information that may be useful in addressing mail to Mike Smith, such as the maximum length of messages he is able to receive, what content types he is able to read, and so forth.

### 6.1.7 Registering Names Nationally and Internationally

Registering names is one of the major unsolved issues in the deployment of X.400 and X.500 systems. The concept of a global directory that encompasses all names and addresses worldwide works well as long as there is also a worldwide naming authority that can administer the name space on such a basis. Unfortunately, establishing this type of naming authority is a political rather than a technical task. While ISO and CCITT provide a common naming structure at the international level, naming and registration authorities still must be established locally in each country. Identifying an organization willing to perform this task at the national level has been difficult at times and is still undergoing changes. Currently, ANSI provides naming and registration services in the United States. Registering with a national naming and registration authority such as ANSI results in merely a paper registration where the name of the organization is recorded and the organization is given a prefix it can use to further subdivide the same space within its own organization. For instance, when Acme registers with ANSI, it would be assigned the name:

```
C=US, O=Acme Corp.
```

All names assigned within Acme would then begin with C = US, O = Acme Corp. In essence, registration with ANSI is equivalent to reserving the name and ensuring that no two organizations within the United States are given the exact same name. This is similar to what occurs in the legal world, when a company registers as a business entity in a particular state or country.

As public service providers roll out commercial X.500 services, they will also act as naming and registration authorities to their subscribers. A company that chooses to register with a public service provider will be assigned a name by that service provider. Registration with a public service provider, however, has greater implications than registration with a national naming authority such as ANSI. Typically, it means that the service provider will maintain an entry for the company in its DSA, and will route queries between that company and other companies. The service provider may have registered its name with the national naming authority; for example:

```
C=US, O=SpeedyNetService
```

If Acme were to register with SpeedyNetService, it would be given a name such as:

```
C=US, O=SpeedyNetService, O=Acme Corp.
```

A corporation therefore has a number of choices about where to register its name:

- It can choose not to register its name with any national or international registration authority.
- It can choose to register with its national naming and registration authority if one exists.
- It can choose to register with a public service provider.
- It can choose to register both with the national naming and registration authority as well as with a public service provider.

Not registering is probably the worst choice. An organization that has not registered is isolated from communicating with the rest of the world. Initially, organizations may prefer not to interconnect their directory infrastructure with the outside world, but they have to realize that if they choose to do so at a later date, the entire naming structure will have to change to add whatever RDNs the organization is assigned when it does register. At that time, every name in the organization will have to add a number of additional RDNs as prefixes.

Registering with the national naming and registration authority or a service provider is a better choice in that even if a company chooses not to take advantage of intracompany communications initially, its naming structure is at least set up to support such exchanges if it later becomes a requirement. The choice of registering with the national naming and registration authority or a public service provider is subjective, and must be evaluated in the context of the company's overall business and information management goals.

In the case of international corporations with branch offices in several countries, two registration scenarios are possible:

- The international company may choose to register only locally—say, within the country where its corporate headquarters are located.
- It may choose to register in every country in which it is doing business and where a registration authority exists.

Figure 6.7 shows how an international firm such as Acme could choose to structure its multinational operations so as to register in only one country and then simply subdivide the international divisions into separate branches that fit under the corporate entity. This may have some short-term advantages in that it can lead to faster set-up times and more control at the corporate level. However, it can be expected to be a short-lived scenario, since as the local branches begin to interwork more frequently with other local businesses it becomes impractical for a user in the United Kingdom to have to always query the DSA in the United States in order to find the e-mail address of an Acme employee located in the U.K. branch office.

The designers of the standard envisioned that international corporations would register their branches in each of the countries in which they have offices. Again, this is very similar to the legal world, in which an international company must

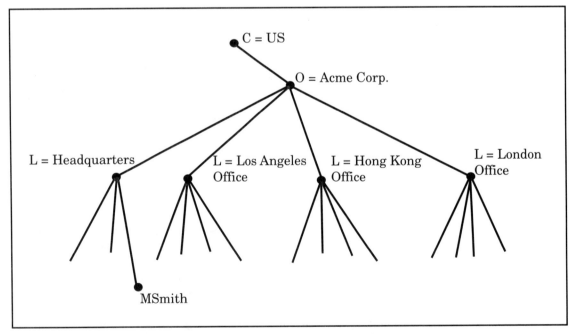

**Figure 6.7** International registration.

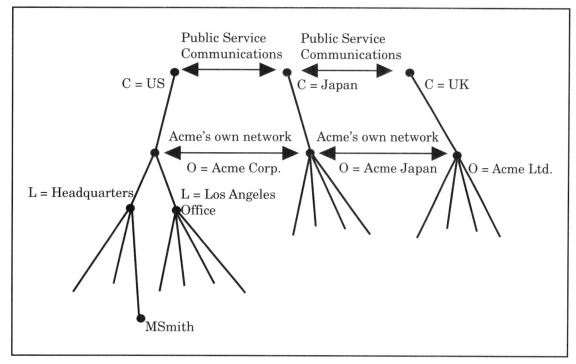

**Figure 6.8** Local registration.

register for business (and sometimes incorporate) in each country where it has offices. Acme could register directly in the United States, Japan, and the United Kingdom. Figure 6.8 shows how Acme would look if it chose to register in every country in which it is doing business.

Under this scenario, communications between the various branches of Acme could take place through public service providers in each country, or could remain a corporate function to be handled entirely within Acme's internal network. In either case, each of the local branches would have names and addresses that could be reached by local queries without needing to route queries through the U.S. branch of the company.

## 6.2 DEFINING CUSTOM ATTRIBUTES AND OBJECT CLASSES

The attribute type and syntax macros defined in Chapter 5 allow implementations of X.500 to define their own custom attributes and object classes. This may be useful in particular industries where there is a need to standardize new kinds of commonly shared data. It is also useful within corporations to expand the kinds of information that can be maintained in the directory to more accurately reflect the needs of business applications within the company. Imagine, for instance, a highly automated automobile manufacturing plant needing to define special attributes to represent factory assembly-line stations and other company-specific information. Most commercial implementations of X.500 will allow users to define their own attributes and object classes, to accommodate the widest possible deployment of the X.500 technology. The user interface and procedures that may be carried out to define such new attributes will vary from implementation to implementation, but in all instances the enabler is the macro mechanism presented in Chapter 5.

Once a company or industry-specific attribute is defined, it must also be registered, and information about it must be made available to all potential users before it can be implemented. There is no way in 1988 X.500 for a user or application to read the directory attributes that are not standard or for which it does not know the semantics. In order to publicize new attributes, it is desirable to register them on a corporate level or on an industry level. Such registration typically involves no more than publishing a paper list of all nonstandard attributes and their definitions. X.500 was defined in principle to support an almost unlimited set of nonstandard attributes. The 1993 extensions to X.500 begin to define mechanisms that will allow users and applications to understand the syntax and semantics of nonstandard attributes directly from the directory through the use of a more sophisticated attribute model (see Chapter 10).

## 6.3 PARTITIONING THE DIT OVER MULTIPLE SERVERS

Once the DIT layout has been designed and agreed upon, the next decision that needs to be made is how it will map to the physical layout of the DSAs. Figure 6.9

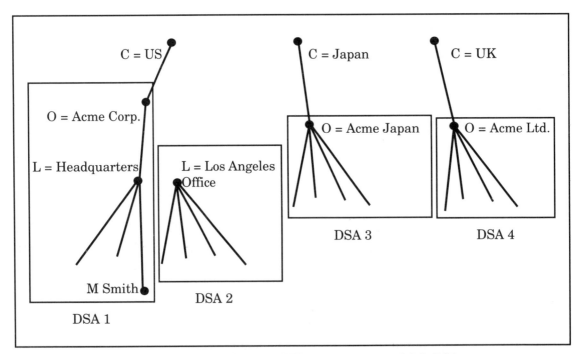

**Figure 6.9** Deploying Acme's DIT structure over multiple DSAs.

shows how Acme's DIT structure would map to physical deployment over multiple DSAs. It shows the headquarters branch of the DIT contained within a single DSA (DSA 1) located at corporate headquarters in New York City, the Los Angeles branch contained within DSA 2 located in Los Angeles, the Acme Japan branch contained within DSA 3, and the Acme Ltd. branch contained in DSA 4. Note that since the entry for O = Acme Corp. is kept in DSA 1, DSA 1 will have to keep a pointer to the subordinate entries of O = Acme Corp. that are held in DSA 2. Chapter 7 will explain what algorithms are used in X.500 to route queries correctly within such a system of DSAs, as well as what pointers each DSA must keep about data stored in other DSAs.

The physical realization of Acme's directory service consists of four DSAs deployed on a worldwide basis, as shown in Figure 6.10. We have simplified things considerably in the example by assuming that all the DIT information at headquarters will fit within a single DSA. Typically, this is not the case, and there may be multiple DSAs holding portions of the headquarter's DIT.

Since DSA 2 is logically subordinate to DSA 1, we can choose to keep the entry for O = Acme Corp. in DSA 1, and to provide access to DSA 2 only through DSA 1. DSAs 1, 3, and 4, on the other hand, either must be fully connected with one another, as shown in the diagram, or there must be at least one communication path among them (it is okay if there is no direct connection between DSA 1 and DSA 4, as long as they can communicate through DSA 3).

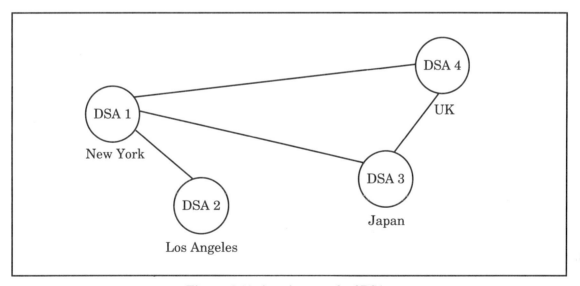

**Figure 6.10** Acme's network of DSAs.

# 7

# The Directory Access Protocol

This chapter provides a detailed explanation of the 1988 X.500 directory access protocol (DAP). It uses an ASN.1-like notation to show in abbreviated form what arguments and results correspond to each operation. Readers who will actually be implementing the DAP protocol will need to move on to a more detailed reading of the standards documents themselves for a complete explanation of each protocol parameter.

## 7.1 DIRECTORY ACCESS PROTOCOL (DAP) SERVICES

The X.500 standards describe the directory service as an object that can be accessed through a set of service ports. Each port is intended to provide a specific set of services, and is identified in the network by a unique access point. Figure 7.1 shows the object-oriented view of the directory service. The access point consists of the name of a DSA and its *presentation address* or network address. According to the OSI upper-layer architecture, each port corresponds to an application service element (ASE).

The 1988 directory access protocol defines three service ports:

- The **ReadPort** provides operations to read directory information, including Read, Compare, and Abandon.
- The **SearchPort** provides operations to search and list directory information, including List and Search.

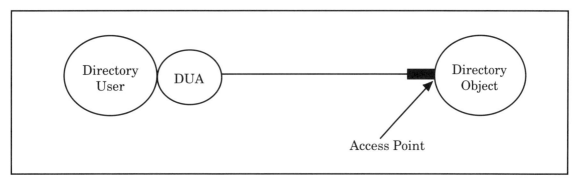

**Figure 7.1** Directory object.

- The **ModifyPort** provides operations to modify the DIB information, including AddEntry, RemoveEntry, ModifyEntry, and ModifyRDN.

Two additional operations, Bind and Unbind, are provided to respectively establish and release an association between a DUA and a DSA. While this separation into distinct service ports seems to imply that DSA implementations need not support all service ports, conformance to the 1988 directory standards does make support of all three ports mandatory. The grouping of functions into service ports as defined in the standard merely provides a convenient way to discuss the functionality of the directory service. The DAP protocol is an application context (AC) constructed by combining the three directory service ports with ROSE, ACSE, and operations to Bind and Unbind associations.

## 7.2 DAP OPERATIONS

Each of the operations of the DAP protocol are described in detail in the section below.

### 7.2.1 Directory Bind

The DirectoryBind operation allows a DUA to establish an application level association with a DSA. The DirectoryBind operation maps onto ACSE's A-ASSOCI-ATE operation, which is used to set up an OSI association between a DUA and a DSA. The bind operation takes as inputs password information and any other security parameters necessary to set up a secure association.

```
DirectoryBind ::=
     ARGUMENT { Credentials OPTIONAL,
                 Versions }
     RESULT { - same as argument - }
     ERROR { SecurityError, ServiceError }
```

The authentication credentials specified in the **Credentials** argument may be simple or strong, as defined in the X.509 authentication framework, or they may be defined as external. External credentials mean that an authentication scheme other than X.509 is being used. The syntax and semantics of such external credentials are defined by an algorithm agreed upon between the DUA and the DSA implementations offline via a mechanism outside the scope of the standard. The **Versions** argument refers to the version of the implementation supported. A bind operation will fail if the DSA does not support the same version as the DUA.

The standard does not define how a DUA locates which DSA on the network to bind to. This can be administratively configured and maintained in a communication profile in the same computer as the DUA. In a LAN network environment it can be obtained by broadcasting out to all servers and waiting for a DSA on the same local network to respond. Often, a mixture of the two methods is used, with the broadcast mechanism providing a back-up in the event that the original DSA specified in the DUA's communication profile is unavailable (for example, if it is down or does not respond).

### 7.2.2 Directory Unbind

The DirectoryUnbind operation is used by a DUA to terminate an association with a DSA. The DirectoryUnbind operation maps on to ACSE's A-RELEASE operation in order to terminate the OSI association between DUA and a DSA.

```
Unbind ::= { }
     RESULT { - same as argument - }
     ERROR { SecurityError, ServiceError }
```

### 7.2.3 Read

The Read operation is used to read information from a single directory entry. It allows the user to read all the attribute types in an entry, only certain specified attribute types, or specified attribute types and their values.

```
Read ::=
     ARGUMENT { name,
                EntryInformationSelection,
                COMPONENTS OF CommonArguments }
     RESULTS { EntryInformation,
                COMPONENTS OF CommonResults }
     ERRORS { AttributeError, NameError, ServiceError,
                Referral, Abandoned, SecurityError }
```

The Read operation takes as arguments the name of the entry to be read, which may be either the fully distinguished name or an alias name, and the **EntryInformationSelection** argument, which is used to request various collections of the information present in the entry. The possible collections that can be requested are:

- The type of each attribute and the value of all attributes (the entire entry);
- The type of each attribute only;
- The type and value information for a specified subset of the attributes in the entry;
- The type information only for a specified subset of the attributes in the entry.

The EntryInformation result conveys the information requested from the specified entry, including:

- The entry's distinguished name.
- Whether the information returned comes from the original entry or a copy.
- The set of requested attribute types.
- The set of requested attribute types and their values.

The Read operation always returns the distinguished name of the entry read, irrespective of whether an alias was used in the original query. This makes it possible to check whether the alias was indeed correctly dereferenced to the intended entry (that we are reading from the correct entry). The **EntryInformation** result also identifies whether the information was read from an entry or its copy. This deals with caching and other replication mechanisms. Depending on the form of replication and the update/refresh mechanism being used, a workstation may place more confidence in information it receives from the original entry than from a copy of the entry that may have been generated by caching or some other form of replication.

### 7.2.4 Compare

The Compare operation is used to compare a *value assertion,* which is a test value specified by the user in the request. The Compare operation was designed to support authentication and security by allowing password verification without having to retrieve the data.

```
COMPARE ::=
     ARGUMENT { DistinguishedName,
                AttributeValueAssertion,
                COMPONENTS OF CommonArguments }
     RESULT { DistinguishedName OPTIONAL,
              matched,
              fromEntry }
     ERRORS { AttributeError, NameError, ServiceError,
              Referral, Abandoned, SecurityError }
```

The **fromEntry** result indicates whether a copy of the actual entry was used. This is similar to the Read operation.

### 7.2.5 Abandon

The Abandon operation is used by a DUA to indicate to the directory that it is no longer interested in the results of an operation. It gives DUAs a way to terminate an operation without having to tear down and reestablish the association. In effect, it tells the DSA that it should discard any results obtained thus far.

```
ABANDON ::=
        ARGUMENT { InvokeID }
        RESULT { NULL }
        ERRORS { AbandonFailed }
```

The **invokeID** argument corresponds to the ROS **invokeID**, which identifies the ROS operation to be abandoned. The Abandon applies only to the Read, Compare, List, and Search operations; that is, those that may involve multiple DSAs in processing the request. Modify operations, such as AddEntry, ModifyEntry, and so on cannot be abandoned.

The Abandon operation is somewhat anomalous in that it is not guaranteed to succeed. For example, a DSA receiving the Abandon request may already have chained the operation to be abandoned onto other DSAs. This makes it very difficult to design a mechanism that will "chase" the original operation and suppress it effectively. The standard states that if an Abandon request is received too late (that is, after a DSA has already propagated the operation to be abandoned onto another DSA), then the DSA receiving the request has two choices:

1. It can propagate the Abandon request if it has implemented some form of proprietary mechanism for suppressing chained Abandon requests, or
2. It can simply ignore the Abandon request and return an Abandon-Failed error.

In either case, the DSA is responsible for suppressing the return of any results of the operation to the requesting DUA since the receipt of an Abandon request always indicates that the DUA is no longer interested in receiving the results of the operation.

### 7.2.6 List

The List operation lists the names of the immediate subordinates of a specified entry. It does not return any of the data held in the subordinate entries themselves other than their names. The list operation will dereference aliases only if requested to do so by the service control settings (service controls are described in Section 7.1.12).

```
LIST ::=
ARGUMENT {DistinguishedName,
          COMPONENTS OF CommonArguments }
RESULTS {
     CHOICE
     ListInfo {DistinguishedName OPTIONAL
               subordinates,
               partialOutcomeQualifier OPTIONAL,
               COMPONENTS OF CommonResults },
     uncorrelatedListInfo }
     ERRORS { NameError, ServiceError, Referral, Aban-
              doned, SecurityError}
```

The **subordinates** result returns information about each subordinate entry, including:

- The RDN of the subordinate.
- Whether the information was obtained from the actual entry or from a cached copy.
- Whether the subordinate is an alias.

The **partialOutcomeQualifier** is returned when the result is incomplete. It may consist of:

- A limit problem, such as size, time, or administrative limit exceeded.
- An **unexplored** indication, in the event that other DSAs necessary to successfully complete the operation could not be contacted.
- An **unavailableCriticalExtensions** indication, in the event that protocol extensions deemed to be mandatory are not supported by one or more DSAs involved in executing the operation.

The **uncorrelatedListInfo** result is used to carry partial results digitally signed by different DSAs. This may occur in a large network environment where different DSAs may be managed by different companies or public service providers and may not have access to one another's authentication keys. In this event, a DSA may receive back digitally signed results from chained queries that it is not able to verify. The standard makes provisions for this case, by allowing such signed results to be passed transparently by the DSA and handed off to the DUA that initiated the query. It is then assumed that the DUA has access to the various authentication keys it needs to verify all the digitally signed results, before collating them together and handing them over to the DUA.

### 7.2.7 Search

The Search operation returns all entries in a specified portion of the DIT that match the specified filter criteria. The operation as input a subset argument, which indicates whether the search should apply only to the base object, to the base object plus its immediate subordinates, or to the base object and all its subordinates all the way down to the leaf nodes of the DIT.

```
Search ::=
ARGUMENT { DistinguishedName,
           subset,
           filter,
           searchAliases,
           EntryInformationSelection,
           COMPONENTS OF CommonArguments }
RESULTS {
     CHOICE
           searchInfo { DistinguishedName,
                        EntryInformation,
                        partialOutcomeQualifier,
                        COMPONENTS OF CommonResults }
           uncorrelatedSearchInfo }
ERRORS { - - same as for List - - }
```

The search filtering criteria, set via the filter argument, can be very broad and may include any of the following settings:

- Equality matching,
- Substring matching,
- GreaterOrEqual or LessOrEqual matching (on attribute values only),
- Present (to verify the existence of particular attribute types), and
- Approximate matches on values based on locally stored expansion algorithms (such as for orthographic or phonetic matching).

Like a Read operation, the Search takes as arguments the name of the base entry at which the search is to begin, which may be either the fully distinguished name or an alias name, and the **EntryInformationSelection** argument, which is used to request various collections of the information present in the entries that match the specified search filter criteria. The possible collections that can be requested are:

- The type of each attribute and the value of all attributes (the entire entry);
- The type of each attribute only;
- The type and value information for a specified subset of the attributes in the entry;
- The type information only for a specified subset of the attributes in the entry.

In performing the Search operation, aliases are dereferenced only if this is requested by the appropriate service controls.

The **EntryInformation** result returns the attributes and/or values from each entry that satisfied the specified filter criteria. The **PartialOutcomeQualifier** and **uncorrelatedSearchInfo** results have the same meaning as described above for the List operation.

### 7.2.8 AddEntry

The AddEntry operation adds a new entry to the DIT.

```
AddEntry ::=
ARGUMENTS { object,
            entry,
            COMPONENTS OF CommonArguments }
RESULTS { NULL }
ERRORS { AttributeError, NameError, ServiceError,
         Referral, Security Error, UpdateError }
```

The **object** argument denotes the distinguished name of the entry to be added. Its superior entry is obtained by removing the last RDN in the object name. The entry argument contains the attribute information that will make up the entry. Upon adding an entry, the directory service automatically checks that the new entry conforms to the schema for the portion of the DIT to which it is added. However, if the entry being added is an alias, the directory will not attempt to verify whether it points to a valid entry (that is, that the entry exists). Aliases are not dereferenced by the AddEntry operation, so it can be used to remove alias entries.

In the 1988 version of the standard, new entries can be added only to the bottom of the DIT hierarchy, which means in effect that only new leaf entries can be created through the DAP protocol. Means outside the scope of the standards, such as proprietary protocols, must be used to add entries anywhere in the DIT or change its structure.

### 7.2.9 Remove Entry

The RemoveEntry operation removes an entry from the DIT.

```
RemoveEntry::=
    ARGUMENT {object,
              COMPONENTS OF CommonArguments }
    RESULTS {NULL }
    FRRORS {NameError, ServiceError, Referral,
    SecurityError, UpdateError}
```

The **object** argument denotes the distinguished name of the entry to be deleted. Aliases are not dereferenced by the RemoveEntry operation, so it can be used to remove alias entries.

In the 1988 version of the standard, only leaf entries can be removed through the DAP protocol. Proprietary mechanisms outside the scope of the standard must be used to remove or change the relative structure of entries within the rest of the DIT.

### 7.2.10 ModifyEntry

The ModifyEntry operation changes an entry's attributes or values.

```
ModifyEntry ::=
     ARGUMENT { object,
                changes,
                COMPONENTS OF CommonArguments }
     RESULT { NULL }
     ERRORS { AttributeError, NameError, ServiceError,
              Referral, SecurityError, UpdateError }
```

The o**bject** argument is the distinguished name of the entry to be modified. The changes argument defines a sequence of modifications to be applied in order. If any individual modifications fail, an **AttributeError** is returned. The directory service ensures that the sum total of changes applied to an entry does not violate the schema for that portion of the DIT. Aliases are not dereferenced by the ModifyEntry operation; it can be used to modify attributes or values of alias entries.

ModifyEntry is not restricted to leaf entries, but can operate on any entry within the DIT, provided that it does not violate the schema definitions for that portion of the DIT.

### 7.2.11 ModifyRDN

The ModifyRDN operation changes the RDN of a leaf entry.

```
ModifyRDN ::=
     ARGUMENT { object,
                newRDN,
                deleteOldRDN,
                COMPONENTS OF CommonArguments }
     RESULTS { NULL }
     ERRORS { NameError, ServiceError, Referral,
              SecurityError, UpdateError }
```

The **object** argument is the distinguished name of the entry whose name is to be modified. The **newRDN** argument is the new RDN of the entry modified. Modifying an RDN also includes adding an RDN component to an existing entry (that is, lengthening an existing name by one more RDN). The **deleteOldRDN** boolean flag indicates whether all attribute values in the old RDN should be deleted. If it is not set, the old values remain.

Aliases are not dereferenced by the ModifyEntry operation, which means it can be used to change alias names.

In the 1988 version of the standard, this operation is restricted to operate on leaf nodes only, since changing the RDN on an internal DIT node implies a change in the DIT structure. In the 1993 standard, this operation was redefined to allow entire subtrees to be moved from one area of the DIT to another.

## 7.3 COMMON ARGUMENTS AND PARAMETERS

This section describes some of the key arguments and results that are common to all DAP operations.

### 7.3.1 Common Arguments

All DAP operations take a number of service control parameters that affect the execution of the operation. These include:

- **Service controls,** which specify a set of constraints on how an operation is to be executed.
- **Security parameters,** which ensure appropriate authentication and security.
- The **distinguished name** of the DUA that initiated the operation.
- The **OperationProgress** argument, which is used to ascertain the progress of distributed operations.
- An **AliasedRDNs** argument flag, which indicates whether the object is the result of an alias that was dereferenced in a previous operation.
- An **Extensions** argument, which supports the inclusion of additional arguments not yet specified by the standard.

### 7.3.2 Service Controls

Service controls are parameters that constrain the execution of an operation. They may be used to set such requirements as:

- **preferChaining**, a request by the DUA to the DSA that the chaining mode be used in executing the operation.
- **chainingProhibited**, a request by the DUA to the DSA that only referrals should be used to carry out the operation.
- **localScope**, an indication of whether the operation should be restricted to operate only within a predefined set of DSAs, such as an administrative domain or a geographical region.
- a **timeLimit** within the operation is expected to return.
- a **sizeLimit** on the amount of data that the operation should return.
- **dontUseCopy,** which indicates that the operation should not return information from copies.
- if **dontDereferenceAliases** is set, aliases are not dereferenced while executing the operation; if it is not set, aliases are dereferenced.
- The standards define the **priority** setting as a way to indicate the relative priority of an operation. Unfortunately, however, there is no way to actually map this to the behavior of the lower-layer OSI protocols and force one operation to be carried out over others. In any case, the presence of the service control can be used at the DUA level to more

effectively manage the return of operation results to the DUA user. For instance, the DUA could be designed to actively interrupt the DUA client upon receipt of results from a query which was previously marked with a very high-priority setting.

- **scopeOfReferral** defines a geographical boundary within which a referral is acceptable, such as a domain, country, and so on.

### 7.3.3 Extensions

The Extensions argument was added to the service controls to support migration to future versions of the standard. It allows additional arguments that are not part of the baseline 1988 standard to be included in an operation. The idea is that two communicating entities may have mutually agreed to use a common set of extensions by means outside the scope of the standard. An identifier is used to identify the semantics of the particular set of extensions. A *criticality subcomponent* is included with all Extension arguments to denote whether a particular extension is mandatory to the execution of an operation or only recommended. If a mandatory extension is not supported by a DSA involved in executing the operation, the operation fails.

### 7.3.4 Security Parameters

Security parameters include the following:

- **certificationPath** contains the sender's certificate plus a possible sequence of certificate pairs. The certificate associates the sender's public key with its Distinguished Name. It is also used to verify digital signatures.
- **name** is the distinguished name of the first DSA to which the operation was submitted.
- **time** is the expiration time of the signature.
- **random** is a random number used in conjunction with the time stamp to detect any replay attacks.

### 7.3.5 Common Results

CommonResults qualifies the information returned by every directory query operation. It is defined by the following ASN.1:

```
CommonResults ::=
    SET { SecurityParameters,
          performer,
          aliasDereferenced }
```

- **performer** is the distinguished name of the DSA that executed the operation. If the results are signed, performer will hold the name of the DSA that signed the results.

- **aliasDereferenced** indicates whether an alias was dereferenced in executing the operation.

### 7.3.5.1 Errors

Most of the errors listed in the preceding sections are fairly self-explanatory. A few errors, however, deserve special mention in X.500.

- **Referral** is not really an error. However, it is returned by DSAs on an operation when the Referral mode of interaction is being used.
- **UpdateError** is used to indicate that the schema definitions for a particular portion of the DIT would be violated if the operation was carried out.
- **Abandoned** is returned when an operation terminates, indicating that the abandon operation was successful.

# 8

# Distributed Operations

Directory services may be either distributed or centralized. In small network environments they are typically centralized, with all the information residing in a single server. This makes administration of the database very simple, and performance measured in terms of response times adequate as long as the number of users supported on the network remains small (on the order of one hundred or fewer users). As networks grow, however, and become geographically distributed, it becomes necessary to also distribute the directory service.

This chapter provides an overview of the key concepts and techniques available in building distributed directory services. It describes in detail how X.500 supports data partitioning, and what information each DSA must keep in order to locate entries in the distributed DIB. It also provides an in-depth look at how name resolution is handled.

## 8.1 X.500 DISTRIBUTED OPERATIONS

In the 1988 version of the directory standards, the DSP provides facilities for locating information in the distributed directory environment, but not for automatically keeping replicas of information up to date. While the 1988 protocols allow the replication of parts of the DIB or the entire DIB through caching, the upkeep and synchronization of replicated information must be done either through proprietary protocols or through other mechanisms outside the scope of the standards. This currently makes interoperability between 1988 DSA implementations from different vendors at the DSP level practically impossible (see Chapter 9). This is an area that has been addressed by the 1992 extensions work.

### 8.1.1 Partitioning of Data

In large OSI networks, the DIB is usually too large to be contained within a single DSA, so it is necessary to partition it over multiple DSAs. As the information within a particular DSA grows, the DSA is said to *delegate authority* to other DSAs for subordinates of any entries it holds. Delegation of authority begins at the root of the DIT and proceeds downward. This simple concept allows individual management domains to maintain a great deal of autonomy over their assigned name spaces. Figure 8.1 shows a DIT distributed over three DSAs. DSA 1 had delegated authority for the sales subtree to DSA 2, and for the R&D subtree to DSA 3. The administrative authorities for DSAs 2 and 3 could choose to further subdivide the name space by placing subordinate entries in other DSAs logically below DSAs 2 and 3.

When the DIB is partitioned in this way, each DSA holds a set of partial subtrees of the DIT, called *naming contexts*. Naming contexts may be of any size, ranging from a single entry to the entire DIT (if the whole DIT can be stored in a single DSA). Naming contexts are constrained by the following rules:

1. They may not span multiple DSAs.
2. They must begin at a vertex and extend downward to either leaf entries or pointers to entries for which the DSA has delegated authority to other DSAs.

Figure 8.2 gives an example of a valid and an invalid naming contexts (as comprised within the enclosing circle). Figure 8.2a represents a valid naming context

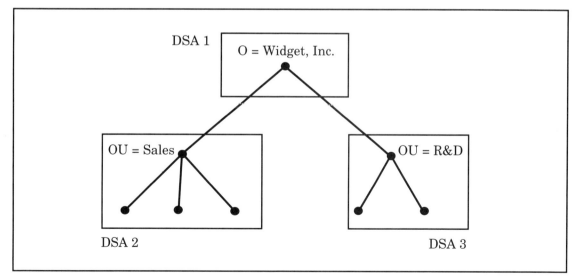

**Figure 8.1** DIT partitioned over three DSAs.

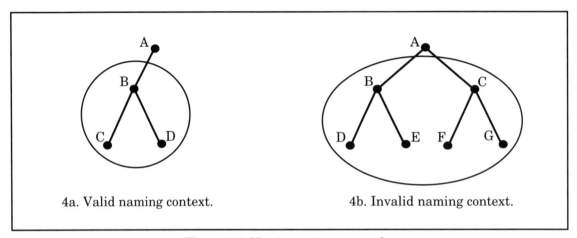

4a. Valid naming context.          4b. Invalid naming context.

**Figure 8.2** Naming contexts example.

because it begins at vertex B, and extends down to the leaf nodes. Figure 8.2b is an invalid naming context since it contains two initial vertices, B and C. The DIT in Figure 8.2b could have been a valid naming context either by including node A in the naming context or by defining two separate naming contexts, one beginning at B and another one beginning at C.

Naming contexts fulfill several needs. By being uniquely identified by the distinguished name of their initial vertex, naming contexts represent a self-contained unit of information. This makes them ideal for replication; a replication protocol can be defined to simply copy a naming context by specifying the name of its vertex.

Figure 8.3 illustrates a DIT partitioned into three naming contexts, distributed over two DSAs. Often a DSA will correspond to a single naming context. However, it is also possible to partition the information contained within a single DSA into multiple naming contexts. This allows different update policies to be applied to each naming context independent of the others.

### 8.1.2 The Knowledge Model

The term *knowledge* is used in X.500 to denote the information that an individual DSA implementation must keep about where information is stored throughout the system of DSAs that make up the directory environment. Many directory systems refer to this knowledge information as the "glue" that holds the directory information together. Knowledge is in effect a set of pointer references that allow DSAs to reconstruct the DIT's logical structure as it is partitioned over multiple DSAs. As we will see in the next sections, the way in which knowledge is defined is tightly coupled to what algorithm is used to perform name resolution (that is, locate information in a distributed directory environment).

1988 X.500 defines three kinds of mandatory knowledge references:

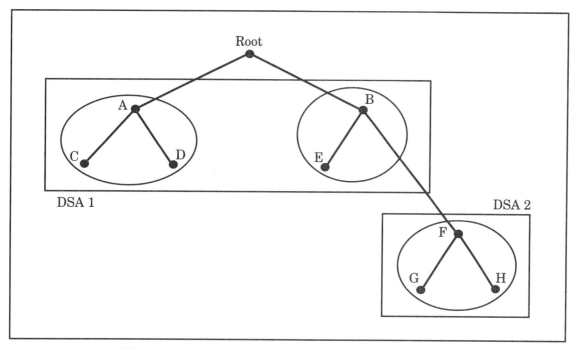

**Figure 8.3** Naming contexts distributed over multiple DSAs.

1. **Internal references** point to locally held entries.
2. **Subordinate references** point to entries for which the DSA has delegated authority to other DSAs. Subordinate references consist of the RDN of the immediate subordinate entry, and the access point of the DSA holding the subordinate.
3. **Superior references** point to a DSA that holds the root of the DIT, or a naming context closer to the root. Superior references consist of the access point of the DSA holding the root, or of the DSA holding the naming context closer to the root.

In addition, two optional kinds of knowledge references are defined:

1. **Cross references** may point anywhere in the name space. Cross references consist of the name of a naming context and the access point of the DSA where it is stored. They are used to optimize name resolution by pointing to DSAs to which queries are forwarded often.
2. **Non-specific subordinate references** (NSSRs) are similar to subordinate references, but do not contain the name of the subordinate RDN. Non-specific subordinate references consist only of the access point of a subordinate DSA. They are in a sense "blind" references to one or more subordinates held in another DSA. Non-specific subordinate references were designed to cater to situations in which a DIT is managed by different administrative authorities and the identity of

information stored in a DSA that belongs to another management authority must be protected. NSSRs are highly controversial, as they complicate considerably the design of the name resolution algorithms. In particular, the standard mandates that multicasting must be used when encountering an NSSR during name resolution.

### 8.1.3 Minimal Knowledge Requirements

To be able to resolve user queries, DSAs must hold the following minimal set of knowledge references:

- An internal reference for each local entry it holds.
- A subordinate reference for each subordinate held in another DSA. This allows queries to be forwarded for continuation in the subordinate DSA.
- A superior reference which is used to route queries up the hierarchy of DSAs until one is found that holds a branch of the DIT that matches an initial subset of RDNs specified in the query.

Figure 8.4 shows a system of DSAs that make up a particular directory environment. According to the above rules, the number of knowledge references that must be maintained by each DSA in the system is very well-defined and bounded to a well-understood number of references. For instance, DSA C in the figure must hold one subordinate reference for each naming context for which it has delegated authority to a subordinate DSA. It also must maintain one superior reference, in this case a reference to DSA A, which is superior to it in the system of DSAs. Finally, DSA C can hold as many cross-references as it deems useful to streamline the name-resolution process by forwarding queries to other DSAs that hold information that is requested frequently.

The 1988 version of the standards does not provide protocol facilities for automatically updating knowledge information. Currently, knowledge references must be updated either through proprietary protocols or by means outside the scope of the standards. This area has been at least partially addressed by the 1993 extensions work.

### 8.1.4 The Root Context

X.500 defines a special kind of naming context called the *root context*. The root context has significance particularly in defining the name-resolution rules at the top level of the DIT structure.

The formal descriptions of the directory DIT mention the root of the DIT. The root of the DIT is a fictional entity; there is no real root, only a set of entities that make up the immediate subordinates of the root.

Whether a DIT is the worldwide DIT or a DIT representing the name space within a company or organization, there are special rules for how information queries are managed at the root of the DIT. Root context is a convenient term to refer to the top-level naming context that contains the immediate subordinates of

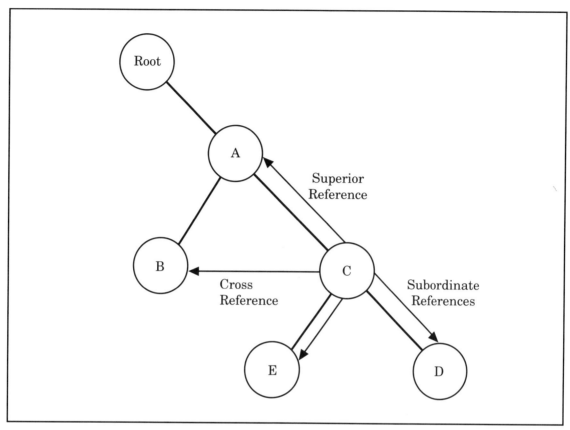

**Figure 8.4** Minimal DSA knowledge.

the root of the DIT. If these immediate subordinates are stored in different DSAs, as is most often the case, then each of these DSAs must contain a knowledge reference to at least one other top-level DSA.

All DSAs containing immediate subordinates of the root must be logically connected to one another in such a way that a query may be forwarded all around the system of DSAs that hold the immediate subordinates of the root. This does not mean that each DSA must connect to all others, but merely that a path must exist through the entire system such that the top-level DSAs are fully connected with one another.

Figure 8.5 illustrates this simple concept for the case of a global DIT where the DSA holding the entry for C = US maintains a knowledge reference to the DSA holding the entry for C = UK, which in turn holds a knowledge reference for the DSA holding the entry for C = Canada. Through this kind of connectivity, a query for a user in Canada can start at a DSA within the U.S. name space and be forwarded for resolution to the U.K. DSA and finally to the Canadian DSA, where it will eventually locate the entry for the specified user.

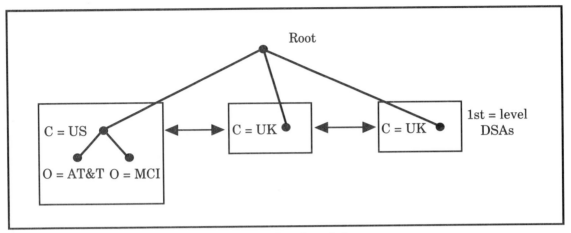

**Figure 8.5** Root knowledge.

## 8.2 NAME RESOLUTION

Name resolution is the process of locating entries in the distributed DIT. Logically, name resolution begins at the root of the DIT and proceeds downward, matching each RDN in a given name to a vertex of the DIT. Name resolution, however, may start at any DSA regardless of its position in the DIT hierarchy. DSAs rely on their knowledge references to appropriately route queries for information they do not hold locally. X.500 defines a highly structured algorithm for performing name resolution, which is guaranteed to converge on the required entry within a well-bounded number of steps. This is particularly important since it assures that directory queries will not be forwarded indefinitely on a trial-and-error basis, but rather will follow a well-defined algorithmic procedure for either identifying the required entry or rejecting the name passed in the query as nonexistent.

The name resolution algorithm in X.500 consists of two procedures:

- **FindInitialNamingContext** finds a DSA that holds the branch of the DIT that matches an initial subset of the name presented in the query.
- **LocalNameResolution** locates an entry within a particular naming context.

Names are rejected as invalid if either of the following circumstances arises:

- An initial naming context in which to start performing local name resolution cannot be found.
- In sequentially matching RDNs to vertices of the DIT, no vertex is found to match a particular RDN.

Figure 8.6 summarizes the name resolution algorithm. (Note: the X.500 standards documents contain a far more detailed flow chart description of the procedure and detailed information on monitoring its progress accurately). In Figure

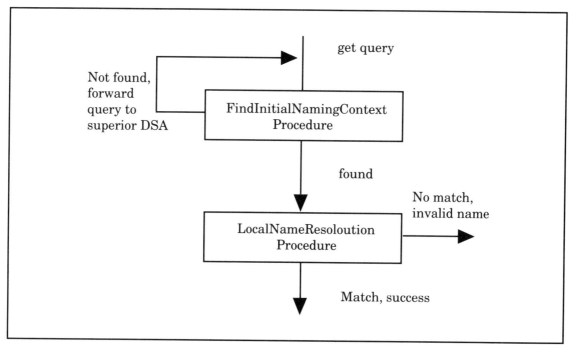

**Figure 8.6** Name resolution algorithm.

8.6, the FindInitialContext procedure is executed until an initial branch of the DIT
is identified that matches the initial portion of RDNs in the distinguished name.
When the correct branch is found, the name resolution process enters the Local-
NameResolution procedure. LocalNameResolution has two possible outcomes—
either all the RDNs in the name match vertices of the DIT, or a match cannot be
found for one of the RDNs specified, in which case the query is rejected as having
passed in an invalid name.

The FindInitialNamingContext procedure shown in Figure 8.7 attempts to
match the initial sequence of RDNs in a given name to a branch of the DIT. It
does so by first trying to match the name to the names of any of the locally held
naming contexts. If no local context prefix is matched, the procedure next attempts to match one of the locally held cross references. If a cross reference is
matched, the query is forwarded to the DSA pointed to by the cross reference,
and the name resolution process continues with the LocalNameResolution procedure. If neither a locally held context prefix is matched or a cross reference is
matched, the DSA uses its superior reference to forward the query up the system of DSAs to a higher-level DSA. The idea is that a superior DSA will have
greater visibility of more branches of the DIT, and therefore is more likely to
identify an initial matching branch when performing the FindInitialNaming-
Context procedure. Whenever a DSA identifies a branch of the DIT that matches
the initial portion of the name specified in the query, the LocalNameResolution
procedure begins.

The LocalNameResolution procedure shown in Figure 8.8 takes over after an

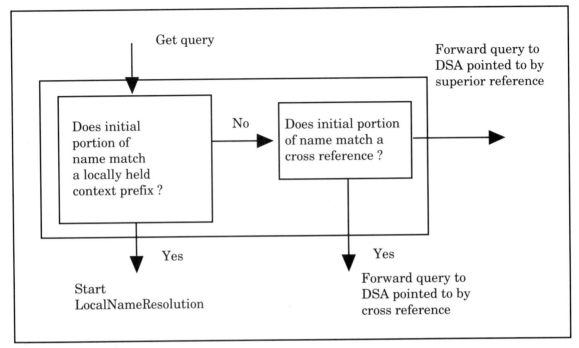

**Figure 8.7** The FindInitialNamingContext procedure.

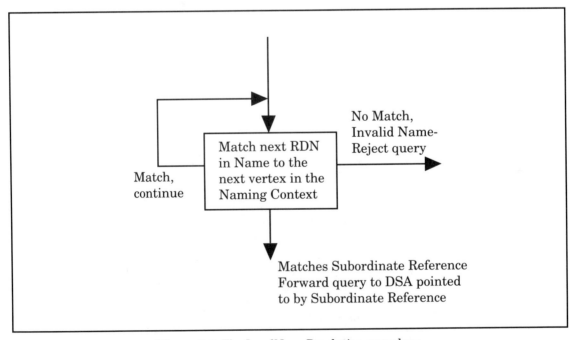

**Figure 8.8** The LocalNameResolution procedure.

initial match is found between the initial portion of the name and a locally held context prefix. The procedure then attempts to sequentially match each remaining RDN in the name to a vertex of the locally held naming context. If at any point in this process the procedure matches a subordinate reference (either a subordinate reference or an NSSR), the query is forwarded to the DSA pointed to by the subordinate reference. The receiving DSA will continue the name resolution process by continuing to match RDNs in the name to vertices it holds. If at any time during the execution of the LocalNameResolution procedure an RDN in the name does not match the next vertex in the DIT structure, the name is found to be invalid and the query is rejected.

### 8.2.1 Examples of Name Resolution

The following section traces the name resolution of two queries in the DIT and system of DSAs shown in Figure 8.9.

In the first example, a query for entry CN = B. Ross is sent to DSA 2. The name specified in the query is the full distinguished name for B. Ross, as follows:

```
{ O=Widget, Inc, OU=R&D, OU=SW Development, CN=B.Ross }
```

1. DSA 2 attempts to match as many as it can of the initial RDNs in the name to locally held naming prefixes. The name does not match any context prefix held in DSA 2. Since the name also does not match any cross references held by DSA 2, DSA 2 uses its superior reference to forward the query to DSA 1.

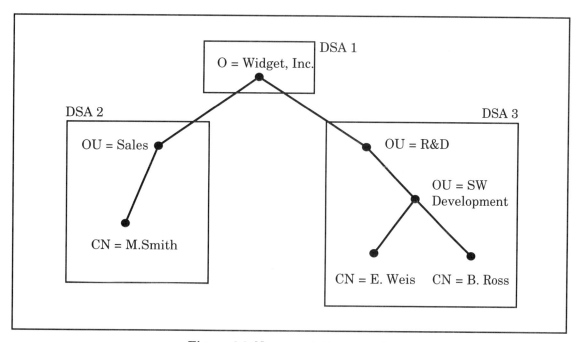

**Figure 8.9** Name resolution example.

2. DSA 1 is able to match the RDN OU = R&D to a subordinate refer-ence to DSA 3. DSA 1 uses the subordinate reference to forward the query to DSA 3.
3. DSA 3 is able to match the query to naming prefix {OU = R&D} and begins to execute the LocalNameResolution procedure.
4. It matches all the remaining RDNs in the name to locally held entries and finally locates the entry:

```
{O=Widget, Inc, OU=R&D, OU=SW Development, CN=B.Ross}
```

At this point, the operation specified in the query is executed, or read, and the re-sults are passed back to DSA 2, which returns the answer to the client DUA.

In the second example, a query for CN = J.Davis is sent to DSA 1. The name specified in the query is the full distinguished name for J. Davis, as follows:

```
{O=Widget, Inc, OU=R&D, OU=SW Development, CN=J. Davis }
```

1. DSA 1 begins to execute the FindInitialNamingContext procedure and is able to match the name to a subordinate reference to DSA 3. DSA 1 uses the information provided by the subordinate reference to forward the query to DSA 3.
2. DSA 3 is able to match the query to naming prefix {OU = R&D}, and therefore begins to execute the LocalNameResolution procedure. In doing so, it is able to match the RDNs OU = R&D and OU = SW De-velopment to locally held entries. However, it is not able to match RDN CN = J.Davis to any entry below OU = SW Development, therefore, the name is determined to be invalid and the query is rejected.
3. The information that the query failed because an invalidly specified name is returned to DSA 1, which passes the result back to the client DUA.

### 8.2.2 Techniques for Optimizing Name Resolution

The definition of name resolution and the requirements for maintaining knowl-edge references are flexible enough to allow for a number of different topology con-figurations between DSAs. In particular, there are a couple of configurations that can be used to streamline name resolution in both small and large network envi-ronments.

Because name resolution is designed to logically begin at the root of the DIT, it follows that some performance savings can be obtained if the root information (i.e., the names of the immediate subordinates of the root) are replicated in each DSA. Each DSA is immediately able to determine whether a branch of the DIT even ex-ists to match a given query. This saves the step of moving up the hierarchy of DSAs to locate the correct DIT branch in which to begin mapping. Also, it is highly likely that the first DSA that receives the query will be able to begin processing it within its locally held naming contexts. Figure 8.10 illustrates a small network composed of four DSAs where the root context is replicated in each DSA.

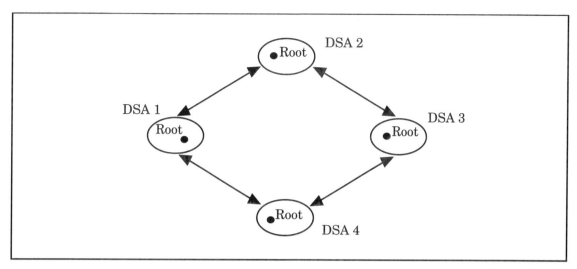

**Figure 8.10** Replicating the root context.

In a large network, on the other hand, it may be desirable to specialize the function of DSAs by placing all the top-level naming contexts (including the root context) in some DSAs and placing all the lower-level naming contexts in others. This type of configuration is shown in Figure 8.11. It turns the top-level DSAs into *query routers* whose primary role is forwarding queries along the system of DSAs. The lower-level DSAs, on the other hand, will typically service user requests directly, or merely forward to their superior DSAs queries that they do not recognize. As the role of the DSAs becomes specialized on the basis of the information stored in them, it also becomes practical to consider employing several platforms with different processing characteristics to implement the different kinds of DSAs. For instance, router DSAs need high processing speed but may not need to maintain a

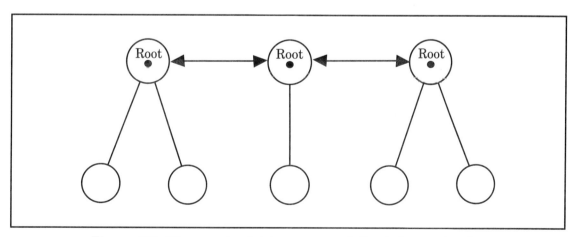

**Figure 8.11** "Query routers" doing name resolution in large networks.

lot of data, therefore, they require smaller disks in favor of increased CPU capacity and increased communications hardware and software capabilities. Lower-level DSAs, on the other hand, would require very high disk capacity and perhaps almost no communications capabilities, except the ability to connect to their immediately superior DSA.

## 8.3 THE DIRECTORY SYSTEM PROTOCOL (DSP)

The DSP is composed of directory service ports similar to those for the nondistributed directory object. These are:

- The **ChainedReadPort**, which includes the ChainedRead, Chained-Compare, and ChainedAbandon operations.
- The **ChainedSearchPort**, which includes the ChainedList and ChainedSearch operations.
- The **ChainedModifyPort**, which includes the ChainedAddEntry, ChainedRemoveEntry, ChainedModifyEntry, and ChainedModifyRDN.

Conformance by DSAs to the 1988 distributed operations protocol is optional. That is, vendors may offer DSAs that support only the DAP protocol (such DSAs either may be used in small networks, where a single DSA is sufficient, or may use some proprietary protocol for DSA-to-DSA interactions). In any case, if a vendor chooses to claim conformance to the DSP protocol, then all of the ports and operations listed above must be supported by the DSP implementation.

Chained operations are constructed simply by adding a set of chaining arguments and chaining results to the equivalent DAP operation. The chaining arguments contain fields to support name resolution and the distributed execution of operations. The chaining results contain additional parameters that are relevant to distributed operations. A *trace field* as part of the chaining argument allows each DSA involved in processing a query to append its name to the operation; this serves to ensure that looping of queries can be detected and suppressed.

Chained operations may be thought of as occurring in two stages:

- A **name resolution** stage, in which the operation is forwarded to the DSA that holds the entry specified in the query, also called the *target object*.
- An **execution** stage, where the target object has been located and the specified operation (read, search, and so on) can begin executing.

The ChainedList and ChainedSearch operations will most likely involve forwarding queries to multiple DSAs for execution. In the case of ChainedList, shown in Figure 8.12, the execution of the operation requires that the query be forwarded to each subordinate DSA that holds an immediate subordinate of the target entry, and that each DSA return the subordinate's name.

In the case of ChainedSearch, shown in Figure 8.13, the query is forwarded down potentially many levels of DSAs to identify all entries that match a particular set of filter criteria. In both instances, where DSAs hold nonspecific subordinate ref-

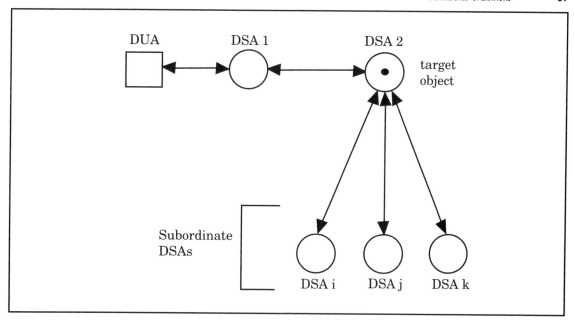

**Figure 8.12** ChainedList execution.

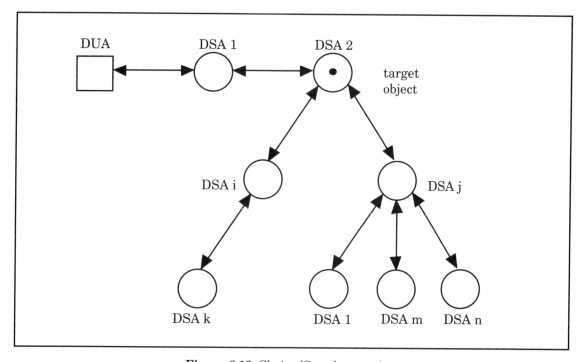

**Figure 8.13** ChainedSearch execution.

erences, the directory mandates that the query be multicast to its subordinates. This kind of multicasting is an application-layer form of multicasting in that it is not time-critical, but rather merely implies that the same request is being sent to multiple recipients in a single transmission. Each recipient then proceeds to execute all or part of the request and return its results within different time-frames.

The 1988 version of the DSP does not yet support the addition and removal of entries across DSA boundaries. Some work was undertaken as part of the 1993 extensions to develop protocols that support this important function.

# 9

# The X.509 Authentication Framework

The X.500 standards define an authentication framework known as X.509, which serves as the basis for providing security and authentication in X.500 directory services. However, X.509 is designed to go beyond the security needs of directory services to provide a generic set of security services that can be adopted by other OSI application-layer services, such as network management, X.400 message handling, and others. Unfortunately, X.509 was a late addition to the development of the 1988 X.500 standards, and the first draft of the standard published in 1988 required major revisions to correct errors and omissions in the encryption algorithms and in some text. Nevertheless, X.509 has become accepted as one of the leading security architectures for use not only within the context of OSI networks, but also throughout the networking industry as a whole. Ongoing OSI standardization work in the area of security is heavily based on the concepts originally defined in X.509.

## 9.1 CRYPTOGRAPHIC TECHNIQUES

Two types of encryption techniques are commonly used to provide security in distributed systems: symmetric and asymmetric. In *symmetric cryptography* (also known as *private key*), the sender and recipient share the same key. Symmetric cryptosystems represent the more conventional form of security. The private key is used by the sender to encrypt information and by the recipient to decrypt the information, as shown in Figure 9.1. Data Encrypton Standard (DES) is one of the algorithms most commonly used to implement a symmetric cryptosystem. Mes-

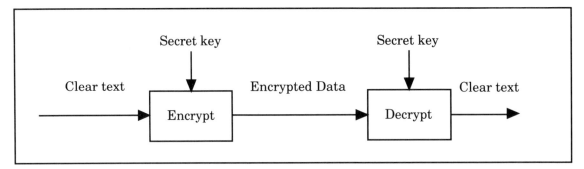

**Figure 9.1**  Symmetric (private key) encryption.

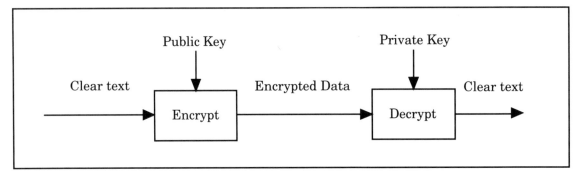

**Figure 9.2**  Asymmetric (public key) encryption.

sage integrity and user authentication are provided by computing a cryptographic checkvalue, called the *authenticator,* over the message using a key shared by both the originator and the recipient. One important aspect of private key encryption is that if the key becomes known, security is compromised.

*Asymmetric,* or public key, cryptography relies on a pair of keys to encrypt information. Each user possesses two keys: a public key, which is available to anyone on the network and serves to encrypt messages destined for that user, and a private key, which is known only by the user and is used to decrypt messages it receives. This is shown in Figure 9.2. X.509 is based on such public key encryption techniques.

## 9.2 THE DIRECTORY MODEL AND AUTHENTICATION

The directory service has a dual role in X.509 as both a user and a provider of security services. The directory service uses authentication and security services to protect the information stored in its databases. It also acts as an authentication service, providing authentication and security to other applications (such as X.400 mail). As a provider of security services, the directory carries out several functions:

- It serves as the repository for authentication certificates, which are packages of authentication information that includes the user's public keys.
- It can also act the network agent that verifies users' authentication credentials and that may be tasked to generate and assign authentication certificates to users and other network services.

The directory is used to store *certified* public keys. The certificates are a package of information which associates the public keys of network users with the user's distinguished name. In the course of carrying out authentication, the certificates are typically read from the directory through the use of the directory access protocol (DAP). The directory service protocol (DSP) may also be used to access certificate information when authentication is taking place between two DSAs.

## 9.2.1 Certificates

Public keys are generally stored in the directory in the form of a package of information called a *certificate*. Certificates are constructed by "signing" (the concept of digital signatures is explained in Section 9.3.4) a set of information that includes the user's name and public key. Certificates are also used to convey a copy of the asymmetric public key of the user to which the certificate pertains. A certificate will typically include the following information:

1. **Signature-Algorithm-ID:** An object identifier that denotes the algorithm that was used to sign the certificate.
2. **Issuer:** The directory name (that is, the distinguished name) of the certification authority that issued the certificate. The certification authority is typically the organization responsible for issuing and managing the certificates. The name of the certification authority may correspond to the distinguished name of a DSA associated with that certification authority.
3. **Validity:** A predefined period of time during which the certificate is considered to be valid.
3. **Subject:** The directory name of the subject of the certificate (that is, the user to whom the certificate pertains.)
5. **Subject-Public-Keys:** One or more asymmetric public keys of the subject of the certificate.
6. **Algorithms:** One or more algorithm identifiers with the public key of the subject of the certificate.
7. **Signature:** An asymmetrically encrypted, hashed version of all the above parameters computed by the certification authority that issued the certificate. It is computed by applying the algorithm used to sign the certificate plus the certification authority's secret key.

Certificate information may be expressed using the following notation:

```
CA <A> = CA {SN, SI, CA, Ta, A, Ap, AI, S}
```

Where SN is the serial number of the certificate, SI is the signature algorithm identifier, CA denotes the certification authority for User A, Ta is a preestablished period of validity of the certificate, A is the user's distinguished name, Ap is the public key for User A, AI is identifies the algorithm used to produce the signature, and S represents the signed data.

Certificates have the following properties:

1. Any user who has the public key of the certification authority can recover the public key of users served by the certification authority. This is because the public key of the certification authority is used to verify the digital signature, which guarantees the integrity of the certificate information held for each user.

2. No party other than the certification authority can modify a user's certificate without it being detected.

Certificates for each user can be held in the directory as attributes contained within that user's directory entry. X.500 defines the following attributes for this purpose:

1. UserCertificate stores each user's public key.
2. CACertificate stores the public key of the user's certification authority.
3. CrossCertificatePair stores the public keys of other certification authorities that may be involved in an authentication exchange between two parties.

The public key of user A can be obtained by any user who knows the public key of the certification authority for user A. A *certification path* is a list of certificates that allows a user to get the public key of another user. Each item in the list of certificates is a certificate for the certification authority of the next item in the list. In this way, a certification path constitutes an unbroken chain of trust among certification authorities, as shown in Figure 9.3.

In the most general case, in order to reciprocally authenticate each other, users must obtain from the directory the complete forward and return certification paths. That is, they must possess all the public keys of the certification authorities in each other's domains in order to be able to access the public key information signed by those certification authorities. A number of useful optimizations, however, are defined to this general scheme. In particular, it can be expected that in most cases, two entities wishing to authenticate each other will share the same certification authority and therefore will not need to rely on certification paths, as both have the public key for the same certification authority.

Where two entities do not share the same certification authority, it is usually simpler for them to exchange, through some offline mechanism, each other's certification authority public key, as well as the public key of any intermediary certification authorities that may be in the communication path between the two entities. Alternatively, certification paths may be stored in the directory and the two entities will rely on a series of directory queries to obtain the full certification

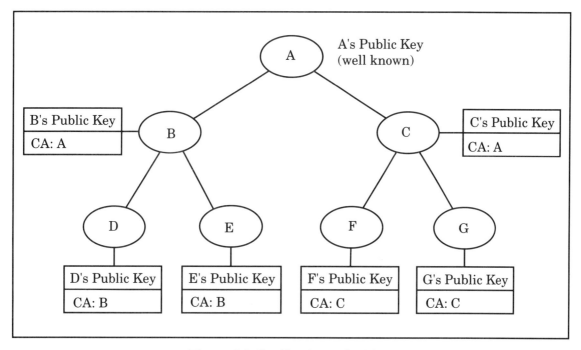

**Figure 9.3** Certification authorities.

path. When this method is selected, implementations are usually designed to cache the results of directory lookups for later reuse.

## 9.3 X.509 SECURITY SERVICES

The directory authentication framework defines three basic security services that are intended to be used by all OSI application layer services:

- Simple authentication,
- Strong authentication, and
- Digital signatures.

Simple and strong authentication allow two application-layer entities to reliably verify each other's identities. that is, they provide for the implementation of mechanisms that unequivocally determine whether a user logging in as Mary Smith is truly Mary Smith and not an imposter. Digital signatures are used in X.500 and in X.400 mail to provide *end-to-end data integrity,* which is a guarantee that information has not been tampered while in transit through the network.

The standards also allow implementations to dynamically register different encryption algorithms by including external ASN.1 definitions. This allows the "grandfathering" of preexisting security schemes, and also the graceful addition of enhanced security schemes in the future.

### 9.3.1 Simple Authentication

Simple authentication is the least secure form of authentication defined by the current standards. However, it is often sufficient in environments where security is not a major concern. X.509 defines three options in support of simple authentication:

Option 1 involves transferring the user's name (typically, the X.500 distinguished name) and a password in the clear. This is a very weak form of security, but nonetheless provides a bare-minimum level of security for low-risk environments.

Option 2 involves transferring a *secure token,* which consists of a collection of data including the user's name, a password, a random number, and a timestamp. The token is protected by a one-way random-hashing encoding function, as follows:

```
f1 (name, Password, r, t)
```

In the function above, $r$ and $t$ are, respectively, a random number and a timestamp indicating when the token was generated. In order for two entities to authenticate each other in this manner, they must share the same hash function.

Option 3 is similar to option 2, but the security token is further protected by a second hash function (denoted as f2). Option 3 is expressed by the function:

```
f2 [ f1 (Name, Password, r,t) ]
```

The use of the second hash function may seem somewhat redundant, but, it increases protection because two entities need to share two similar hash functions, not than just one, in order to communicate.

In option 1, user A sends his or her name and password in the clear to user B. User B queries the directory to check that the password it received from A matches the one held in A's directory entry. The UserPassword attribute type is defined to store user password information within directory entries. If the comparison succeeds, the directory confirms the validity of A's credentials to B. B, in turn, conveys the success of the operation to user A. If the comparison fails, B conveys a failure indication to user A. Figure 9.4 summarizes the sequence of operations.

In option 2, the set of exchanges between user A, user B, and the directory are very similar to those defined in option 1. However, the information exchanged is better protected through the use of a one-way hash function. In this case, user A generates a token called Protected1, which is derived by applying the one-way hash function to the following information: A's name, A's password, a random number, and a timestamp. Protected1 is defined by:

```
Protected1 = f1 [ t1, r1, Name, Password ]
```

Protected1 can then be used to create an authentication token, called Authenticator1, which is defined as:

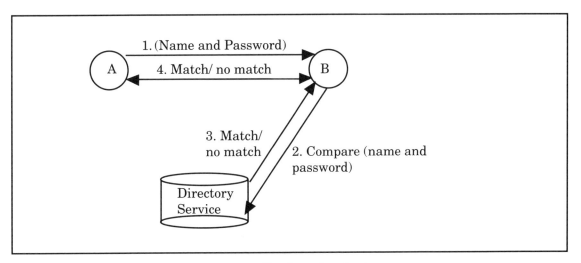

**Figure 9.4** Simple authentication.

```
Authenticator! = [ Protected1, Name, t1, r1 ]
```

User A sends Authenticator1 to B, which uses the information contained in Authenticator1 to reconstruct Protected1. User B queries the directory to obtain user A's password, and hashes the password with the user name values, r1 and t1, which it received from user A. If the result matches Protected1, then the authentication has completed successfully and user B notifies A of that; otherwise authentication has failed.

In option 3, the sequence of events is largely the same as in option 2, with the addition that Protected1 is hashed further with a second has function called f2, in order to yield Protected2. Protected2 is defined by the following function:

```
Protected2 = f2 [t2,r2 Protected1]
```

Authenticator2 is defined as:

```
Authenticator2 = [t1, t2, r1, r2 Protected2]
```

Again, user A sends Authenticator2 to user B, which reconstructs its value locally with information it read from the directory as well as information it receives in the token.

### 9.3.2 Strong Authentication

The X.509 strong authentication scheme is based on public key encryption. While the standard does not mandate a particular encryption algorithm, the RSA (named after its designers Rivest, Shamir and Adleman) algorithm is heavily implied. RSA is a public key (or asymmetric) cryptosystem. It mandates that each entity have two keys; a public key and a secret key. RSA has the property that both keys can be used for encryption. If the secret key were used to encrypt the information, the public key would be used to decrypt it, and vice versa.

Public keys need to be stored in a central repository accessible to multiple entities in the network; the directory is an ideal repository. There is no need to protect public keys. A sender who wishes to send information to a recipient in a secure manner obtains the recipient's public key from the directory and uses it to encrypt the information. The encrypted information is then sent to the intended recipient, who will decrypt it using the secret key.

X.509's strong authentication scheme is specified as a point-to-point scheme, based on the notion of an unbroken "chain of trust." The concept of a chain of trust works as follows: if DUA A trusts DSA 1, and DSA 1 trusts DSA 2, then DUA A trusts DSA 2 (see Figure 9.5).

Clearly, if the security of DSA 1 is broken, then the chain of trust is broken. Unfortunately, relying on a chain of trust does not work well in a distributed environment. It is fairly obvious to realize that any DSA can be tampered with, thus invalidating the entire chain of trust. Nevertheless, X.500 specifies point-to-point authentication mainly as a way to provide authentication between DUAs and the directory service as a whole, as shown in Figure 9.6. There is a strong underlying assumption that within the directory environment itself, security either is not a concern or is provided for through a variety of means outside the scope of standardization. End-to-end security in the directory is currently provided for only through the use of digital signatures, which guarantee end-to-end data integrity and implicitly allow verification of identity of the sender and the recipient.

### 9.3.2.1 Strong Authentication Procedures

Authentication information is exchanged between two parties when an association is first set up at bind time. Authentication information is exchanged by two communicating entities through the use of the bind operation arguments, and is mapped onto the mechanisms provided by ACSE for the secure transfer of authentication information. Once an association has been successfully established, additional protection may be provided through the use of digital signatures that guarantee the integrity of the request and result information exchanged over the association.

X.509 defines three possible exchanges for strong authentication: a one-way exchange, a two-way exchange, and a three-way exchange.

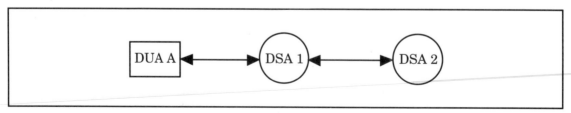

**Figure 9.5** Unbroken chain of trust.

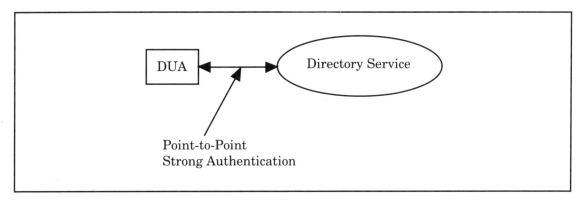

**Figure 9.6** DUA authentication.

In the one-way authentication exchange, a single transfer from entity A to entity B establishes the identity of A and that the authentication token originated at A. By implication, it also establishes the identity of B and the integrity (and nonreplay) of the authentication token that was sent from A to B. Two-way authentication is similar to one-way, except that entity B sends a reply token back to entity A. The reply token establishes in a more reliable manner the identity of B. The three-way authentication is similar to the two-way authentication, but relies on a third exchange between A and B to supplant the need for timestamping the tokens. The three-way authentication is therefore less dependent on mutually synchronized time clocks, which is important because OSI lacks a synchronized time protocol. However, the three-way exchange cannot really be used with ROSE-based protocols, since it does not fit well with ROSE's two-way request-reply style of exchange. The three-way authentication exchange is defined in the standard more for the sake of full generality than with the expectation that it will really be adopted in ROS-based systems such as X.500 and X.400.

### 9.3.3 Digital Signatures

Digital signatures provide the basic mechanism of ensuring data integrity. Information is signed by appending to it an enciphered summary of itself. The summary can be produced by means of a one-way hash function, which guarantees that false information cannot be substituted. A mutually agreed-upon hash function must be used between sender and recipient in order to implement digital signatures.

The encipherment of information is carried out by using the secret key of the signer. This guarantees that digital signatures cannot be forged. The digital signature function is summarized as follows:

```
X {Info} = Info, Xs [h(info)]
```

where Info represents the information to be signed, Xs is the secret key of the signer, and h is the hash function.

The recipient of signed data can perform the following steps to verify the validity of the signature:

1. Apply the one-way hash function to the information, and
2. Compare the results obtained with the results obtained by deciphering the signature using the public key of the signer.

## 9.4 Generation and Management of Key Pairs

The administrative process required to generate and distribute key pairs is, of course, outside the scope of the international standard. However, the standard does establish some general guidelines for the secure management and generation of key pairs. In particular, it states that key pairs may be produced through any of the following means:

1. A user may generate his or her own key pair, so the secret key is never released to foreign entities.
2. The keys are generated by a secure third party, in which case they must then be transferred to the user in a secure manner.
3. The keys are generated by the certification authority (typically, the certification authority is synonymous to the directory). In this case, a secure data transfer to the certification authority is not necessary, but is needed to transfer the secret key to the user.

Since a certificate associates a user's name with a public key, the certification authority must be reliably sure of a user's identity before generating a certificate for that user. The certification authority must also take care not to issue certificates for two users with the same name. Since the certificate stored in the directory is public, no security is necessary to transport it to the directory.

Certificates are valid only for a predefined time period, after which they expire and must be removed from use. The certification authority is responsible for the timely replacement of certificates that have expired, as well as for issuing certificates in such a way that they do not all expire at the same time. Since timestamps are based on coordinated universal time, some clock synchronization is required. Certification authorities must also be able to revoke certificates prior to their expiration date in the event that a certificate is found to have been corrupted.

# 10

# The 1993 Extensions

In an effort to bring the 1988 CCITT study period to a close within the prescribed four-year study cycle, the designers of 1988 X.500 were forced to make some hard decisions about the scope of the first round of recommendations. The result was that the 1988 version of the X.500 standards lacks a number of critical pieces of functionality required to build truly interoperable, distributed, enterprisewide directory services. In particular, it did not provide standardized support for access controls or a full set of replication protocols to support the automatic synchronization of remote replicas of the database. Initial product offerings based on 1988 X.500 have had to define proprietary mechanisms to support access controls and replication.

The 1993 study period has focused entirely on addressing these missing pieces of functionality by defining a set of extensions to the 1988 X.500 standards. This chapter provides a brief overview of that extensions work (published in 1993 and therefore often also referred to as the *1993 extensions* or the *1993 edition*) and examines what impact it is likely to have on the implementation and deployment of X.500 directory.

## 10.1 WHAT IS MISSING FROM 1988 X.500

The major items that were not dealt with in the 1988 X.500 standards were: replication, access controls, schema, and knowledge management. The lack of each of these features has had a different impact on the development of 1988 X.500 products, and has contributed to slow-down the commercial deployment of X.500 services.

While the 1988 standards permit the existence of copies of DIT information, they provide no automatic support for updating information once it has been replicated. The lack of replication protocols in 1988 X.500 has meant that vendors building distributed directory services have had to design their own replication protocols. In fact, most of the distributed enterprise directories currently available implement the standard DAP and DSP protocols as mandated by 1988 X.500, along with a set of proprietary extensions necessary to support replication.

This is clearly less than was originally desired when the X.500 work began. However, it is also true that at least initially there will be little need for directory service agents (DSAs) from different manufacturers to exchange data. At least during a transition period; incompatible replication protocols from different vendors is tolerable. Nevertheless, as enterprise directories grow it will become increasingly necessary in large distributed environments to have compatible replication protocols.

In the case of access controls, the 1988 situation is simply embarrassing. The standards define a complex and articulate framework for authentication (X.509) that has formed the basis for work on security and authentication in both ISO and CCITT, while at the same time leaving the issue of access controls completely unresolved. Unfortunately, authentication without access controls is of little value— that is, it matters little that authentication proves that Joe Smith is truly Joe Smith if there isn't also a standardized mechanism to decide whether or not Joe Smith has the right to read the corporate personnel files. Defining authentication mechanisms without also standardizing a set of access-control policies and mechanisms has left the issue of security in X.500 directories wide open. Needless to say, security is a paramount concern for most corporate users and government agencies implementing distributed directory services.

Vendors releasing X.500–based products have dealt with this situation by implementing simple forms of proprietary access control mechanisms to go along with their implementation of the X.500 standard. Again, this results in incompatible products from various vendors. Lack of standard access controls makes interoperability among products from different vendors even more difficult than does the lack of replication protocols. The only way that a DUA from one manufacturer today can successfully query a DSA from another is if the access controls parameters are turned off. Clearly, this is an impractical scenario in most production environments.

Knowledge management is closely tied to replication, and refers to the ability to manage the information that the directory service holds internally to help it keep track of how information has been partitioned among multiple directory servers. This internal directory information is used to locate information in response to user queries. Clearly, as DSAs are added or removed from a network, it would be highly desirable for the directory servers in the network to automatically update their knowledge information to reflect the new disposition of the information database. With the 1988 version of the standard, these changes must be tracked and executed manually. This means that in 1988 implementations of X.500, system administrators are typically required to track changes to the knowledge information and rely on offline mechanisms to update each DSA's internal knowledge references. Interoperability between products is not as heavily affected as in the case of replication or access controls, as each product comes with its own configuration mechanisms. Though it is a considerable nuisance for system administrators to rely on different tools and procedures for different products, it does not impact the operational behavior of the distributed directory environment as far as the user is concerned.

Some less significant items also dropped out of 1988 X.500, such as distributed entries and operations acting on multiple entries. *Distributed entries* are entries made up of information that resides in different database servers. The need for such entries is an issue dear to many public service providers (PTTs), which envision the need to distribute large amounts of information describing national services and computing resources across multiple directory servers. While the 1993 study period made some attempts to deal with the need for this feature, it ended up postponing the design of a mechanism to support distributed entries to later study periods.

The need for operations acting on multiple entries, on the other hand, was not revisited at all in 1993, as it was generally felt that for the most part, the same functionality could be achieved through the use of the Search operation as originally defined in 1988 X.500.

## 10.2 THE 1993 EXTENSIONS TO X.500

The 1993 extensions to X.500 primarily address three areas not covered by the 1988 standards for directory services. They are access controls, replication, and schemas.

However, in addressing these three major areas of functionality, the designers of 1993 X.500 realized early on that a common thread exists among them and that the information model defined in 1988 X.500 is not sufficient to accurately model some of the functionality required to describe the internal behavior of the directory service.

This realization led to the development of the 1993 Extended Information Model, which provides the mechanisms necessary to more clearly describe the internal behavior of the directory.

The development of the new information model has had a pervasive effect on all parts of the X.500 standard, and has resulted in addenda to nearly all of the documents that comprise the original 1988 standard. Fortunately, for the most part these changes are of an additive nature and should not seriously hamper migration from the 1988 to the 1993 edition of the standard.

The 1993 Extended Information Model forms the basis for the design of access controls, replication, and schema in 1993 X.500. It specifies that there are two distinct *views,* or models, of directory information.

1. **The User Information Model** corresponds to the attributes and object classes as were originally defined in the 1988 version of the standard.
2. **An Operational and Administrative Information Model** defines a new set of facilities necessary for modeling 1993 information.

The intent of the Operational and Administrative Information Model is that it can be overlaid over the 1988 User Information Model without replacing it or making it obsolete. This means that 1988 protocol operations should still work when directed at 1993 DSAs, and 1993 DUAs will be able to query 1988 DSAs. The difference is that 1993 protocols are also able to query and modify administrative information that is not accessible in 1988 implementations.

The 1993 Information Model relies on two new concepts in order to model information that is specific to the directory service's own internal use. They are *operational attributes* and *subtrees*.

Operational attributes are similar in structure to regular attributes, but are intended to be defined for use by the directory service only. That is, they are not visible through ordinary user queries. It is envisioned that in 1993 X.500 directory entries will have both user attributes, as were defined in 1988 X.500, and operational attributes as defined in 1993. Operational attributes will be used to store information such as access control permissions, knowledge information, and schema information which defines the allowable superior/subordinate relationships of entries in the directory. The new directory entries will therefore comprise, 1988 naming and user attributes, as well as a number of operational attributes necessary to store information required for the directory's internal operation, such as the access controls that pertain to that particular entry, or the name and address of the DSA that holds the master copy of the entry. Figure 10.1 shows a typical 1993 directory entry.

Operational attributes can be associated with single entries, individual attributes, attribute values, or collections of entries, or *subtrees*.

Operational attributes are further specialized into three categories:

1. **Directory operational attributes** may be used to model features such as access controls.
2. **DSA-shared operational attributes** are used to model the information that DSAs will need to make available to other DSAs in order to carry out replication functions.

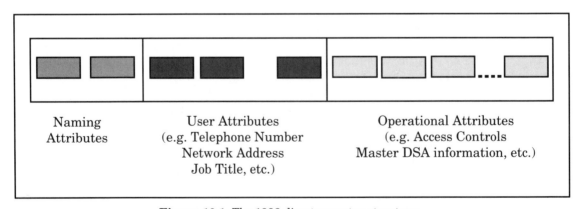

**Figure 10.1** The 1993 directory entry structure.

3. **DSA-specific operational attributes** serve to describe operational information that is specific only to a particular DSA implementation, such as the last time it received an update from the master DSA.

Subtrees are another very powerful concept in 1993 X.500. They denote dynamic subsets of DIT information. They may overlap, and span DSA boundaries. In particular, they can be defined dynamically by specifying an initial entry, a set of boundary entries, and a set of filtering criteria that can be used to include or exclude entries on the basis of the information they contain. The use of subtrees and operational attributes in 1993 X.500, for instance, makes it possible to associate access controls with entire subportions of the directory information base.

Figure 10.2 illustrates the use of subtrees and operational attributes. The entry "XY," for example, may contain a subtree definition that encompasses all the entries within the dotted frame. The subtree definition will be represented within entry XY as a set of operational attributes of which only the directory service is aware. A set of access controls can also be stored at entry XY, again as a set of operational attributes that will have effect on the entire subtree defined at XY. Since the 1993 operational attributes can be manipulated just like any other attribute,

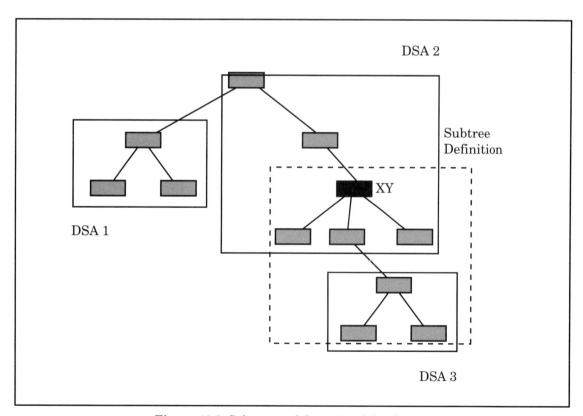

**Figure 10.2** Subtrees and Operational Attributes.

the scope of the access controls stored at XY or their semantics can be changed easily through protocol operations.

### 10.2.1 Access Controls

While authentication serves to verify a user's identity and may also be used to verify the origin of information received, access controls are used to restrict access to information on the basis of identity. The 1993 extensions work defines a set of mechanisms to support access controls based on access control lists. The 1993 X.500 provides a mechanism whereby different access control schemes are dynamically "bound in," provided both cooperating parties can agree on which access control scheme to use. This means that future access control schemes can be defined and used in conjunction with the 1993 protocols, and that current proprietary access control schemes can continue to be used in conjunction with the new 1993 protocols, thus easing product migration. Future study periods are expected to define additional forms of access controls based on more sophisticated mechanisms such as capabilities.

The 1993 list-based access control scheme is called *basic-access-control*. The basic-access-control scheme may be used to protect entries or operational attribute information, including access control information itself. Items that may be protected via the basic-access-control scheme include entries, attributes, and attribute values. Access control information stored as operational attributes may be associated with entries, attributes, or entire subtrees. User classes may be associated with the access control permissions to denote groups of users who may or may not have access to particular pieces of information.

### 10.2.2 Replication

The 1993 X.500 relies on a strict master/shadow model of replication. That means that updates can be directed only to the master of the information. However, indirect shadows—that is shadows of shadows—are allowed. A DSA may be a master for some portions of information while being a shadow DSA for other portions of information.

Replication in 1993 X.500 relies heavily on the use of operational attributes to represent knowledge information, such as superior and subordinate references, as well as master/shadow relationship information.

Replication in the 1993 version of the standards caters to two basic requirements of directories—availability of information and increased performance—by ensuring that data that is often accessed is located close to the DUA making the request. The 1993 version of the standards will support two forms of replication: caching, and shadowing of information. Caching is already available in 1988 directories, and allows DSAs to keep copies of information, but provides no guarantee that it is up to date. Shadowing, on the other hand, involves a contract between two DSAs whereby a master DSA ensures that shadow DSAs receive updated copies of information on an agreed-upon schedule.

The 1993 standards continue to adhere to the principle of transient inconsistency in that they do not require all shadow copies of information to be updated simultaneously. Updates can be directed only to the master of the information, which is then responsible for updating the shadow copies. Access control information is replicated along with the information it protects to ensure consistency of service throughout the DIT.

Two new protocols are defined to handle replication in the 1993 extensions:

1. The directory information shadowing protocol (DISP), and
2. The directory operational binding management protocol (DOP).

The DOP is used between any two DSAs that are entering into an association agreement, either to shadow each other's database information or to keep reference pointers (that is, knowledge information) to each other up to date. Two DSAs must enter into an operational binding agreement through the use of the DOP protocol before the DISP protocol can be used to replicate and update information among them. The DOP protocol allows DSAs to negotiate the nature of the binding agreement and any parameters that will govern the association, such as the frequency with which update information will be sent from the master DSA to the shadow DSA.

The DISP protocol is used between shadowing DSAs to transfer information from one DSA to another, as well as to transmit updates. Since the DISP protocol may have to transfer very large amounts of information among DSAs, it was believed that it should support a reliable bulk data transfer mechanism to ensure the correct delivery of the information. The remote transfer service element (RTSE) protocol already used in X.400 to support message transfer agent (MTA) MTA-to-MTA transfers has been chosen, optionally, to provide the underlying bulk-data transfer facility necessary to implement the DISP.

### 10.2.3 Lack of Knowledge Update Protocols

The 1993 replication work has focused almost entirely on the shadowing aspects of replication, and only begins to address the requirements for updating knowledge information through the provision of the DOP protocol. Clearly, any two DSAs holding knowledge references that point to each other (or from one to the other) must be engaged in an operational binding agreement. However, the existence of an operational binding agreement alone does not ensure that changes in knowledge information are automatically propagated to all the DSAs affected by the change. It is expected that the topic of knowledge management will be addressed in future study periods.

### 10.2.4 Schema

The 1988 X.500 introduced the concept of schema, which are rules that define the permitted relationships between entries of different object classes. The overall intent behind schema rules was to avoid inappropriate structuring of directory information such as placing the name of a country underneath the entry for a person's name. The idea was to have agreed-upon structure rules by which the entire directory database would abide, thus making it easier to search for particular types of information. In the 1988 X.500, however, schema are only a concept; while examples are given, no hard-and-fast mechanisms are provided to describe schema relationships and how schema rules are to be enforced.

In 1993, operational attributes are used to represent schema information as well. Through the use of operational attributes, scheme rules can be represented as attributes contained within directory entries, and can therefore be read and modified to reflect the structure of the information base. Storing schema definitions within the directory as operational attributes allows schema definitions to control the modification of the directory information base and ensure that a consistent structure is maintained.

## 10.3 MIGRATION FROM 1988 TO 1993, X.500

The best news about the 1993 X.500 extensions is that for the most part they are fully backward-compatible with 1988 X.500. The new information model augments the 1988 information model rather than altering it substantially. Best of all, it is still be possible to use 1988 DAP protocols to query a 1993 directory, and vice versa.

The interesting question becomes: To what extent will vendors discard the proprietary extensions they have developed for 1988 X.500 in order to adopt the 1993 extensions into their products? This is of particular interest where key features such as access controls and replication are concerned, as these ultimately affect interoperability between products from different manufacturers.

It can be expected that since 1993 access controls are visible to the DAP protocol user, it is likely that vendors will be highly motivated to adopt the new 1993 access control scheme as soon as possible in their products. One of the primary goals of vendors of directory services is to allow their DSA databases to be queried from the DUAs of any vendor.

That the 1993 access control scheme is designed to allow the dynamic binding of any access control mechanism will make it easier for vendors to develop a smooth transition plan for phasing out their proprietary 1988 access control mechanisms in favor of 1993 access controls. It can be expected, however, that proprietary access control schemes will continue to exist alongside the newly defined standard access controls for a long time to come.

The 1993 replication extensions, on the other hand, are likely to find their way much more slowly into vendors' products. Like access controls, the 1993 replication protocols can be implemented alongside the 1988 DSP protocol, and therefore also do not present a major migration problem. Figure 10.3 shows how the 1988 protocol structure of DAP and DSP can essentially remain in place while being augmented with the 1993 protocols to provide replication. Vendors wishing to incorporate the new 1993 replication protocols into their architectures need not replace the 1988 DSP protocols entirely, but can choose to simply run the new DOP and DISP protocols alongside a 1988 DSP.

However, most vendors have already implemented proprietary versions of the DISP and DOP protocol. Since the pressure for interoperability between DSAs

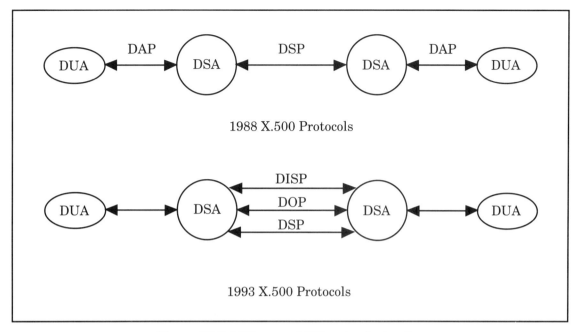

**Figure 10.3**  1988 versus 1993 protocol migration.

from different manufacturers is significantly smaller than that for DUA-to-DSA interoperability, it is less likely that vendors will rush to throw away their proprietary replication protocols in favor of the DPO and the DISP. In addition, both the DOP and DISP protocols are as yet wholly untested. Developing fully interoperable versions out of the 1993 protocol specifications will take several years of testing and experimentation before yielding implementations that are adequate for commercial deployment.

Vendors will gradually replace their proprietary replication protocols with the 1993 replication protocols. Unfortunately, this means that interoperability between DSAs from various manufacturers will continue to be an issue for some time to come.

## 10.4 DEPLOYMENT OF THE 1993 EXTENSIONS

The 1993 access control extensions are likely to be the first and most prevalent aspect of the 1993 extensions work to be implemented both commercially and in research. While it can be expected that proprietary access control schemes will continue to be around for many years to come, they do not allow the level of interoperability that users demand.

As far as replication goes, there is perhaps less value in the 1993 DOP and DISP protocols. From a technical standpoint, these protocols do not offer a level of functionality superior to that which is already being provided by proprietary replication protocols. Also, in most cases the proprietary implementations currently being deployed are based on extensive experiences with preexisting replication technology that has been tested and refined far beyond the 1993 protocols. These proprietary protocols are likely to be much more robust and to yield far better performance than an implementation of the yet-untested 1993 replication protocols. Nevertheless, the principal reason for implementations to adopt the 1993 replication protocols will be to provide interoperability at the DSA-to-DSA level.

## 10.5 REMAINING TECHNICAL ISSUES IN X.500

The 1993 X.500 recommendations go a long way to address areas of functionality not adequately covered in the 1988 version of the standards. There are still, however, a few areas of functionality that are not addressed by the X.500 standards and that may affect how X.500 technology is deployed in the near future. It is also likely that some of these areas will become the subject for design work in the future versions of the X.500 standards (in 1996 or in any accelerated-procedure work items before then).

### 10.5.1 Bulk Operations

As mentioned earlier, directory operations can at times require the transfer of very large amounts of data in both one-to-one and one-to-many data exchanges. Activities that are likely to require support for some kind of bulk data transfer include:

- Replication,
- Updating of large portions of the DIT, and
- Search operations involving large portions of the DIT.

No real thought has yet been given in X.500 to how to support bulk data transfers. The 1993 version of the standards provides for the optional use of the RTS protocol to support the exchange of very large amounts of data when doing replication. RTS is the mechanism already employed in X.400 message handling to support the transfer of large messages. However, the use of RTS in the context of X.500 seems rather an afterthought, and its use is left as an option when sending shadow updates across the network.

It is likely that future versions of the X.500 standards will investigate more extensively the design and use of bulk data transfer protocols for X.500 operations.

### 10.5.2 Transient Inconsistency

The 1993 standards will continue to adhere to the principle of transient inconsistency in that they will not require all shadow copies of information to be updated simultaneously. The standards do require, however, the means to propagate update information to a potentially large number of DSAs worldwide in a timely manner. The adoption of transaction-based update protocols (which ensure simultaneous updating of all copies of information) while desirable in certain respects, makes it difficult to deploy X.500 directory services over different kinds of communication media. Transaction-based update protocols, for instance, would not be suitable for handling updates over satellite media, which introduces appreciable transmission delays.

### 10.5.3 Character Sets

The 1988 X.500 standards have come under a great deal of criticism for supporting a limited range of character set options that do not adequately reflect the international requirements of directory services. The X.500 currently does not support non-Latin alphabets, which makes its deployment on a worldwide basis problematic and has led to some unpleasant political debates. It is expected that future study periods will address this more aggressively, as it has become a very emotional issue in a number of technologically advanced countries where the national language is not based on the Latin alphabet.

### 10.5.4 Batch Operations

The current X.500 protocol operations are designed to operate primarily in the request/reply mode provided by ROS. There is no provision currently to issue a set of request for execution and to collect results at a later time. Each operation must be issued separately and will return upon successful or unsuccessful completion. However, in the context of replication it is possible to envision a requirement for updates to occur offline, where perhaps multiple updates are scheduled to occur at some predetermined time of day. Batch operations are desirable in certain situations where the communication links are costly or difficult to come by and it is desirable to batch up as much of the data traffic as possible for transfer at predetermined times.

# 11

# X.400 MHS Use of X.500 Directory Services

---

The need for X.500 directories was determined during the definition of the 1984 X.400 standards. X.500 is largely a creature of X.400, as the primary impetus behind its definition comes from a desire to provide better support for naming and addressing in large distributed message handling systems.

Since the use of X.500 directory services is optional in 1988 X.400, alternatives have been defined in the standard in order to handle most important functions even without an X.500 service on the network. This is true, for example, of distribution lists (DLs), which may operate both in conjunction with, and in the absence of, X.500 directory services. In general, however, when X.500 directory services are present, functions are handled more elegantly and transparently from the point of view of the user. The expansion of DLS, for instance, becomes much more effective in the presence of a distributed and replicated directory service that allows the DL membership information to be available consistently from all parts of the network (assuming, of course, that a directory entry exists for all members of the DL). This chapter describes the use of X.500 in conjunction with X.400 message handling systems.

## 11.1 X.500 IN THE X.400 MODEL

Figure 11.1 shows how X.500 directory services fit into an X.400 environment. Directory services may be accessed independently by any number of functional components, including message transfer agents, user agents, access unit message stores, and even directly by the X.400 end-user. These entities will typically query

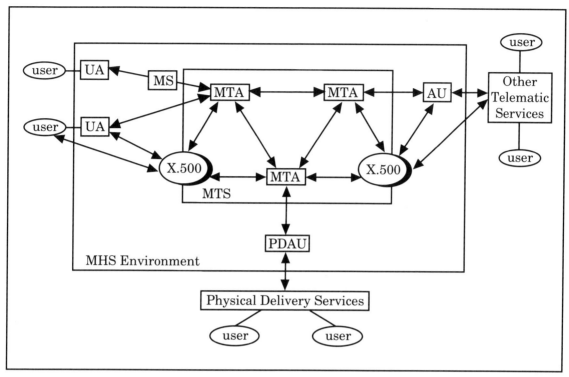

**Figure 11.1** The 1988 X.400 environment.

the directory to perform name-to-address translation as well as to acquire necessary additional information regarding particular X.400 users and resources.

The 1988 X.400 relies on X.500 directory services to provide the following:

- Naming and addressing,
- DL expansion,
- Authentication and security services, and
- Capability assessment.

The X.500 DUA component may be colocated with either the X.400 user agent (UA) or the X.400 message transfer agent (MTA), or both.

Figure 11.2 illustrates how a UA and DUA capability may be colocated to best serve the needs of an X.400 user. The UA can rely on the colocated DUA capability to query the directory and find the originator/recipient (O/R) address information and any relevant capability information associated with a given directory name. The UA may also query the directory, again through the local DUA component, to browse through its information base. Finally, the UA may rely on the DUA to access the directory to perform authentication and validate an intended recipient's credentials.

Figure 11.3 shows how the DUA functionality can be colocated with an MTA on the same mail server. The MTA will use the DUA capability to query the direc-

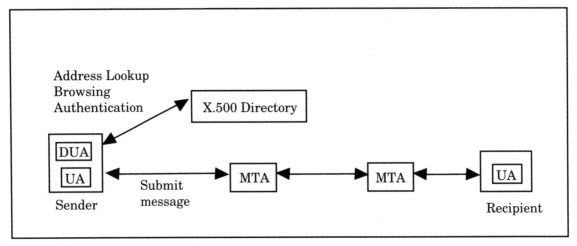

**Figure 11.2** UA use of X.500.

tory in order to determine the capabilities of the recipient UA before attempting message delivery to it, to look up its presentation address and perform password verification, and to expand any DL information that may be present in the list of intended recipients of the message. When DLs are nested, it is possible that several MTAs will progressively need to query the directory to expand the nested DL information in the course of transferring the message. In most network environ-

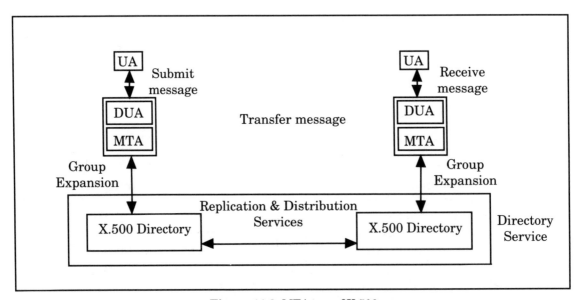

**Figure 11.3** MTA use of X.500.

ments, DUAs will be colocated with UAs and MTAs so that both may avail themselves of directory services.

### 11.1.1 Naming and Addressing

In 1988 X.400, O/R names can consist of a directory name, an O/R address, or both. Directory services may be used by UAs, MTAs, and X.400 users themselves. A directory name is merely one possible component of an O/R name. For simplicity, 1984 X.400 defined O/R names to be equivalent to O/R addresses; 1988 X.400 seeks to make use of directory services to provide O/R names that are distinct from addresses. X.500 names are composed of an ordered sequence of attributes that largely reflect the actual name of the X.400 user or application, and also provide some notion of its place in an organization or geographical location.

In order to obtain an O/R address, the directory service user queries the X.500 database by providing a name (either an alias or the distinguished name) and requesting the corresponding network address. If only the directory name is present when the user submits a message for delivery, the X.400 accesses the directory to obtain the correct O/R address, which it then uses to route and deliver the message. If the directory name is absent, the X.400 relies on the O/R address as given. When both the directory name and the O/R address are present, the X.400 uses the O/R address directly (without further directory lookups). However, the directory name is carried with the message and presented to the recipient along with the O/R address. If the O/R address proves invalid at any stage in the message transfer and delivery cycle, the X.400 can rely on the directory name to match it to an appropriate, valid O/R address.

Where an X.500 directory is present on a network, X.400 will use it to resolve X.500 names and to return the corresponding O/R address. If an X.500 service is not available, X.400 will use the O/R address as specified in the original recipient's name. For an interim period, while X.500 services are still not widely available, it is likely that some users and DLs will continue to rely on 1984-style O/R names based on O/R addresses. Recommendation X.402 provides a set of standard attribute types and syntaxes from which valid O/R addresses may be constructed.

### 11.1.2 Capability Assessment

Beyond simply resolving directory names to O/R addresses, the directory also serves as an invaluable repository of information about X.400 users and resources. As such, it is used in X.400 to discover the intended recipient's capabilities, since these may affect successful message delivery. Any user, UA, or MTA can directly obtain information about the capabilities of an intended recipient by querying the directory. The directory stores all capability information relevant to message delivery in the form of attributes. The following directory attributes are defined for use in representing particular capabilities of X.400 users:

- X.400 deliverable content length,
- X.400 deliverable content types,

- X.400 deliverable encoded information types (EITs), and
- X.400 preferred delivery methods.

The following directory attributes are defined to represent message store capabilities:

- X.400 supported automatic actions,
- X.400 supported content types, and
- X.400 supported optional attributes.

### 11.1.3 Distribution Lists

Distribution lists provide the ability to address a message to a group of users by specifying a single name. The use of DL's is optional in X.400, and is provided by its underlying message transfer system. DLs are a great convenience to X.400 users because they allow users to address a message to a potentially very large group of recipients without having to list each one individually. In many instances, a user will not even need to know the names of all the users with in a particular DL. DLs may be nested; that is, a DL may itself be a member of a larger DL.

Distribution lists are implemented in the directory as entries whose content attributes hold the names of the members of the DL. The name of the entry corresponds to the name of the DL. DLs are identified by means of X.500 distinguished names. DLs may be nested indefinitely through a recursive use of attribute definitions. When an X.400 user, UA, or MTA attempts to address and route a message to a DL, the message transfer service (MTS) queries the directory to obtain the list of attributes contained within the DL's entry. Generally, in a well-designed replicated and distributed X.400 environment, this kind of name-resolution is handled by the MTA transparently. Depending on the size and complexity of the DL, the first MTA involved in a message transfer may be able to completely resolve all the members of the DL. When a DL contains multiple nested DLs, several MTAs may need to progressively query the directory to obtain the full set of DL members.

Replication and distribution of directory information makes it possible for DL information to be accessed from anywhere within the network. This makes it possible for X.400 users to move about the network and still continue to utilize the X.400 facilities from different locations with the same ease of use and transparency.

DL's are characterized by the following properties:

1. **A set of members** consists of users or names of other DLs that are members of the DL.
2. **A DL submit permission** may be a list of users or other DLs that are allowed to send messages to this DL.
3. **A DL expansion point** is the O/R address of the MTA (or domain) where the DL can be expanded; that is, where the full list of DL members is contained. If a distributed directory is used on the network, this information is no longer necessary.

4. **A DL owner** is the name of the user or set of users who manage the DL. The owner is typically responsible for adding users to and removing them from the DL, as well as modifying submit permissions.

DL names are indistinguishable from other O/R names. They may consist of a directory name, an O/R address, or both. A user need not be aware that an O/R name refers to a DL, nor does it need to know whether more DLs are nested within a DL name that it is using. A message originator, however, may set an indication upon message submission requesting that any DLs contained in the recipient name not be expanded. This may be done to avoid unnecessary processing when the originator knows that a number of nested DLs are present, but is interested only in the top-level DL members.

A DL's properties may be stored and managed through the use of the directory service; the DL's name corresponds to the object name, and a set of attributes is used to represent each of the DL properties listed earlier. This is the preferred way to support the implementation of DLs, since the directory's replication capabilities make it possible for DLs to be more easily expandable from any point of origin in the X.400 system.

# 12

# Deployment of X.500 Directories

This chapter looks at issues dealing with the commercial deployment of X.500 technology. It provides a brief overview of the Quipu/ISODE work, which is one of the earliest and most thoroughly tested implementations of X.500, and discusses the evolution of X.500 technology to deployment over non-OSI protocol stacks such as TCP/IP. It discusses the emergence of X.500-like directories, such as Novell's NetWare 4.0 and the commercial deployment of X.500 services by public service providers.

## 12.1 ISSUES IN THE DEPLOYMENT OF X.500 SERVICES

Commercial deployment of X.500 directory services has been relatively slow for a number of reasons:

- Incompleteness of the 1988 X.500 standard,
- Slow deployment of and X.400 and X.500 by public service providers,
- Widespread installed base of proprietary directory services, and
- Slow acceptance of OSI.

While the X.500 technology was long-awaited by the industry as a major step forward in distributed directories, the 1988 version of the standards unfortunately fell short of many of its original goals (see Chapter 10). The lack of major pieces of functionality in 1988 X.500 affected the implementation of products by vendors, as well as production deployment by users.

Also, the existence of a multitude of proprietary directory-service designs has slowed down the acceptance of a single unifying technology. Vendors and users with large investments in products that depend on proprietary designs are not eager to move on to new technologies. Even where there is a strong commitment to standards, product migration is slow, as it involves not only changing the directory design itself but also changing the entire network application infrastructure around it. Migration to a new directory technology is invariably a complex and costly undertaking.

Nevertheless, X.500 technology is a viable integrating directory technology. Though it does not often make sense to abandon the entire installed base of products in favor of X.500, X.500 will eventually provide enterprisewide corporate directory services. Building backbone X.500 directory services (usually in conjunction with backbone X.400 messaging services) provides a cost-effective, scalable, flexible solution to enterprise directory services.

Figure 12.1 illustrates the concept of backbone X.500 directory services. It shows a number of proprietary directory services and address books linked into a common X.500 corporate directory service. Such a corporate directory service will typically be part of an organization's X.400 message handling backbone infrastructure. Proprietary directory services will continue to exist at the local level, but the information they maintain will be integrated into a common corporatewide directory service based on X.500 technology.

## 12.2 ISODE AND QUIPU

The ISO Development Environment (ISODE) is a development effort that was undertaken by a number of U.S. and European researchers in the late 1980s to ex-

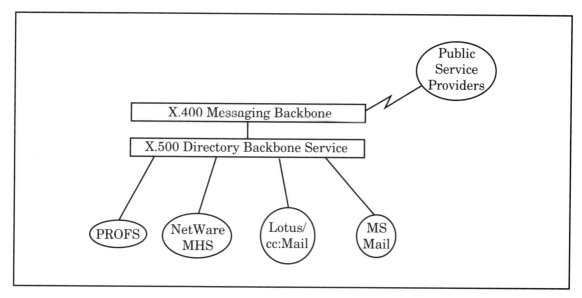

**Figure 12.1** Backbone X.500 directory services.

periment with the deployment of OSI upper-layer protocols. ISODE is an implementation of OSI upper layers, including: Session, Presentation, RTSE, ACSE, ROSE, and a set of ASN.1 handling tools. The ISODE environment also provides implementations of FTAM (File Transfer Access and Management), VTP (Virtual Terminal Protocol), X.400, and X.500 applications. A unique aspect of ISODE is that it is designed to operate over either an OSI or a TCP/IP communication protocol infrastructure. It operates over TCP/IP by mapping OSI application-layer protocols over TCP/IP as defined by RFC 1006.

ISODE was originally in the public domain. This changed with the formation of the ISODE consortium (see Appendix B). The ISODE consortium plans to evolve the ISODE code base in a controlled fashion, which will make it more suitable for commercial deployment. However, an unsupported version of ISODE will continue to be available free of charge on the Internet (by downloading it via anonymous FTP, or writing to the appropriate university distribution sites in the United States or Europe).

The X.500 component of ISODE is called *Quipu* (from an ancient Inca word). Quipu is readily available as part of the ISODE implementation package. It originated as a proprietary directory design and has since evolved to a full implementation of the X.500 standards. Today, Quipu is acknowledged as one of the best-tested experimental deployments of X.500 technology.

Like most implementations of X.500 technology available today, Quipu augments the X.500 standards with proprietary extensions in areas that were left unspecified by the 1988 standards. Quipu adds its own protocol mechanisms for access controls, replication, synchronization, and schema definition. The information model and behavior of the DUA-to-DSA protocols, however, are those specified in the X.500 standards. Although there exists no good benchmarks for what constitutes X.500 compliance, Quipu can be considered to be fully X.500-compliant.

Quipu is widely used today in research networks experimenting with the OSI protocol suite as a whole or studying the area of directory services. In particular, research is underway in a number of universities and other institutions in the use of directory services as full databases that can store extensive amounts of data, including images and other information not directly related to simple name and address lookups.

### 12.2.1 Commercial Deployment of the Quipu Technology

Quipu is also being widely deployed commercially. A number of leading computer vendors have adopted Quipu as the initial foundation for their directory-services product architecture. However, most have found that to date, significant re-engineering work is required to turn the Quipu code into a full-fledged commercial product.

One of the main technical drawbacks of the original Quipu design was its underlying database structure. The designers of Quipu noted that the hierarchical database structure mandated by X.500 resembles very closely the UNIX file structure. In order to streamline their efforts, the Quipu developers decided to rely on the UNIX file system as the underlying directory database. Since UNIX files are arranged hierarchically, the hierarchical relationship that is required to model the DIT is already present. While this type of implementation is simple to realize and administer in a research environment, it is wholly impractical for any kind of production environment, and has yielded poor performance and proved extremely wasteful of system resources. All commercial vendors who have used Quipu as the basis for their product implementations have had to replace Quipu's use of the UNIX file system with a true database. This is typically major surgery, and can require a good deal of time and effort to implement. One of the principal tasks of the ISODE Consortium (see Appendix B, Section 9, for more information on this organization) has been to redesign Quipu to either utilize a high-performance special-purpose database or rely on commercially available database products.

There are, however, some major advantages to vendors' using Quipu as their starting point. First, it provides a first-pass implementation of a system that is one of the most thoroughly tested implementations of X.500 technology available today. It can save many valuable work hours of initial design and prototyping. Nevertheless, Quipu is only a prototype; it still needs significant re-engineering before it can be deployed commercially.

The fact that Quipu has added proprietary extensions for access controls, replication, and some other features also provides some significant advantages:

1. It means that vendors do not have to design these features from scratch.
2. By adopting the extensions as defined in Quipu, vendors have a greater chance of interoperability with products from other vendors that have also started with the Quipu design (changing the database structure does not alter the protocol behavior).
3. The Quipu extensions have already undergone a thorough testing and are known to work and scale well in large distributed environments spanning hundreds of DSAs around the world.

For vendors that choose not to use Quipu as the starting point for their product implementation, Quipu still represents a valuable vehicle for interoperability testing, and fills the need for a reference implementation of X.500 directory technology. For users seeking to deploy X.500 technology within their organizations, Quipu provides a quick introduction to a working X.500 implementation.

## 12.3 X.500 OVER TCP/IP

With Request for Proposal (RF) 1006, the Internet Activities Board (IAB, see Appendix B) specifically defined a mapping for OSI Transport Class (TP0) to the Internet transport protocol, TCP/IP. RFC 1006 emulates TP0 so as to provide any OSI application the necessary OSI transport services. This allows X.500 directory services (as well as X.400 message handling services) to be deployed over a TCP/IP transport stack rather than over the original OSI transports defined by ISO/CCITT. Many of the commercial implementations of X.500 in use today rely on this approach to deploy X.500 in a TCP/IP networking environment. Most com-

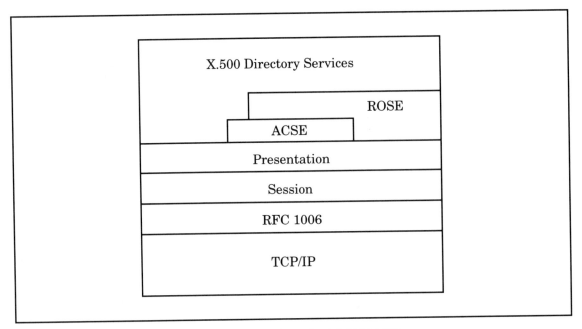

**Figure 12.2** X.500 stack with RFC 1006.

mercially available X.500 products support both the ISO/OCCITT-mandated OSI stack and the RFC 1006 over TCP/IP stack configuration.

RFC 1006 consists of two parts: TP0 and a packetization protocol that separates the TP0 data as it is sent over the TCP data stream. RFC 1006 is a logical transport-to-transport mapping. It does not map from the application layer (layer 7) directly to the transport layer (layer 4). See Figure 12.2. The latter mappings can perform better, but are not interoperable with other types of mappings. This is explained in more detail below.

RFC 1006 emulates OSI LAN transport protocol and services through a simple transport-to-transport level mapping. Transport-level mapping defines the specific protocol and service mappings, without knowing anything about the information being carried by the transport. The emergence of transport application programming interfaces (APIs), such as AT&T System V Transport Library Interface (TLI), has facilitated transport-independence through the availability of XTI and TLI over non-OSI transports. In fact, similar mappings to an alternative transport that map TP0 over Novell's IPX, SNA LU6.2, and so on are being defined by other consortiums and standards bodies. The only requirement placed on the destination transport is that it must provide the functionality of a connection-oriented transport service.

It should be stressed that there are alternative ways to run OSI applications, such as X.500, over TCP/IP networks. One must be careful to make sure the mapping used does not assume knowledge of the transport data itself, by specifically altering how the application data is encoded or encapsulated. Typically, mapping from the application level (layer 7) directly to the transport level (layer 4) assumes and requires very specific application-data encoding and encapsulation. Improper mapping definitions can result in noninteroperable systems. If a translation does not have a transport-to-transport mapping, but rather application-to-transport (layer 7 to layer 4) mapping, then the mapping on the sending and receiving ends must be identical in order for the systems to interoperate.

Several other RFCs exist for mapping specific OSI applications over TCP/IP. These can have certain advantages, but typically will not interoperate with an OSI transport or a RFC 1006 implementation. RFC 1006 will interoperate within all OSI and TCP/IP networks, and also across OSI and TCP/IP networks.

## 12.4 X.500-LIKE PRODUCTS

A number of products have emerged recently that can best be called "X-500-like." X.500-like directories are products that adopt some of the key characteristics of X.500 but do not adopt the ASN.1-based protocol encoding of standard OSI X.500. For instance, such products may adopt a full X.500 attribute and information model, as well as all the protocol behavior of X.500 (that is, the full DAP and DSP protocols). While X.500 was originally designed to operate on top of an OSI stack within the context of an OSI architecture, the emergence of an OSI networking infrastructure is still far behind. For this reason, many vendors are redesigning X.500 to operate on top of non-X.500 protocol stacks. Documented procedures already exist for implementing OSI applications on top of TCP/IP protocols, for example. More important, leading LAN vendors such as Novell are also deploying X.500-like products within their own protocol environments (such as SPX/IPX).

X.500-like products are not protocol-conformant with X.500, as they do not exchange protocol information according to X.500 ASN.1 encoding rules. Their protocol behavior is similar to that of X.500, but the protocol exchanges follow proprietary formats. While this approach may initially seem to invalidate the goal of interoperability, it represents a valid migration approach and ultimately makes it easier to design gateways and gateway agents between different X.500-like directory services and fully conformant X.500 directory services based either on an OSI stack or an OSI-over-TCP (via RFC 1006) stack.

### 12.4.1 Netware 4.0 Directory Services

Novell's NetWare 4.0 directory service is a prime example of an X.500-like directory service. NetWare 4.0 includes a full, distributed directory service called NetWare Directory Services (NDS) in the baseline operating system. NetWare 4.0 represents the high end of Novell's product line, and is intended to meet the specific needs of large enterprise networks. NDS, the directory service component of NetWare 4.0, is specifically designed to meet the long-range needs of growing enterprise networks that require sophisticated directory capabilities to support an increasing base of distributed applications, including network management, groupware, calendar/scheduling applications, workflow automation, and many others.

Two aspects of NDS make it a significant development for the industry:

1. It is based on an X.500 architecture.
2. The fact that it is bundled as part of the baseline NOS environment.

### 12.4.1.1 The NDS Architecture

NDS adapts as much of the X.500 directory services technology as makes sense operationally within a LAN environment. For instance, rather than run X.500 services over an OSI stack, or even over a TCP/IP stack, NDS operates over SPX/IPX protocols. The design of the directory database, naming model, and server-to-server interactions, however, are exactly as in X.500. In addition, NDS supports a published set of APIs that are closely aligned with the X.500 DAP protocol. Where the 1988 X.500 standards were lacking in definition, Novell has extended the X.500 specification to include a number of proprietary extensions for access controls, replication, and authentication and security.

### 12.4.1.2 NDS APIs and Backward Compatibility

NDS is fully backward-compatible with the current NetWare Bindery. NDS has developed an additional proprietary API, which is closely aligned with the X.500 DAP protocol. The NDS API also provides some additional extensions to support authentication, access controls, and replication. In order to remain backward-compatible with NetWare 3.x applications, NDS supports full emulation of NetWare Bindery service calls. This allows existing NetWare Bindery applications to transparently access the NDS service through the old-style bindery calls, which provides a transition strategy whereby applications will gradually migrate to use the full-service interface provided by NDS's new APIs.

Figure 12.3 shows the NDS architecture as made up of database component which can be accessed by two distinct servers: the NDS server which responds to X.500-like client server requests and a Bindery emulator which responds to old-style Bindery calls. In this manner, both old-style Bindery and new NDS-based network applications can transparently access the common information database.

### 12.4.1.3 Transport Protocols

NDS is designed to run over an SPX/IPX stack. It will also operate with any other transport that can be used in conjunction with SPX/IPX, such as TCP/IP tunneling.

### 12.4.1.4 Information Model

NDS is based on the X.500 data and attribute model. It supports a hierarchical database structure.

The naming structure in NDS is almost identical to X.500 distinguished names, but uses periods (.) as separators between fields, whereas X.500 does not define any specific characters as separators. NDS also defines some additional naming attributes types not found in X.500, such as SA to denote a street address. Nei-

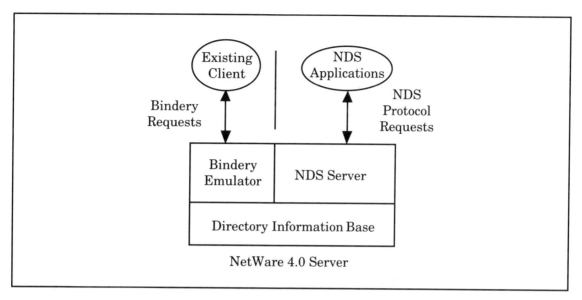

**Figure 12.3** NDS architecture as seen by applications.

ther of these additions impacts interoperability with X.500 directory services, as X.500 itself allows for the provision of locally defined attributes.

### 12.4.1.5 Replication

NDS is a fully distributed and replicated directory service. Replication in NDS follows a master/shadow model just as it does in the specification for 1992 X.500. However, the data replication and synchronization protocols are based on Novell's own proprietary designs, as no framework was available in the 1988 X.500 standards.

### 12.4.1.6 Authentication

NDS provides full support for authentication services based on both private and public key mechanisms. Novell has licensed the RSA public key encryption technology, and NDS is designed to provide support for both private and public key encryption.

### 12.4.1.7 X.500 Compatibility

There are essentially two dimensions for evaluating directory services compatibility:

1. The protocol level; that is, two systems are compatible if they are able to exchange packets on the network without a gateway.
2. The application level; that is, if applications designed to access one directory service can also understand the semantics of the other directory service.

NDS is not compatible with X.500 at the protocol level since it does not follow ASN.1's basic encoding rules (BER) or the OSI protocol-formatting conventions. However, it is compatible with X.500 applications at the application programming interface level.

In order for an NDS server to communicate with an X.500 server, there must be a gateway between the two that can translate protocol requests from one format to the other. Figure 12.4 shows the role of a gateway that supports protocol-to-protocol interaction between NDS and X.500 directory services. Conceptually, the gateway may be thought of as being placed between NDS and an X.500 directory service. The gateway encodes NDS protocol requests into an equivalent X.500 request complying with ASN.1 BER encoding rules, and forwards the request to the X.500 service. In real terms, the gateway may be physically colocated with either the NDS server or the X.500 server.

When seen from the standpoint of applications, NDS can be considered compatible with full X.500 directory services. That is beause the NDS API is functionally identical to the XDS API (which was developed by X/Open and the X.400 API Association specifically for X.500). Even though the definition language is different, it is very easy to design an API translation layer that maps between XDS and the NDS API function calls, or vice versa. Figure 12.5 shows the close correspondence of function calls between XDS and NDS. The XDS API today is supported by most leading vendors of X.500 products.

There are also, of course, a number of functions specific to each API that have been designed to handle the administrative and housekeeping needs of the API data structures. In the case of XDS, these include facilities to allocate API data structures and manage the workspace. For NDS, they include a set of sophisticated procedure calls that are provided to set and modify access control rights, define or modify schema rules, manage replication, and change authentication and security credentials. Some differences do exist in specific argument settings and service controls between the two APIs, but these are fairly minor.

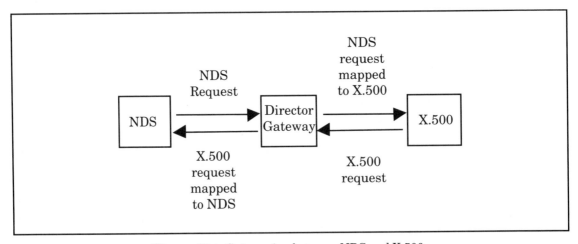

**Figure 12.4**  Gatewaying between NDS and X.500.

| X.500 Operations | XDS | NDS |
|---|---|---|
| Read operations | Read ( ) <br> Compare ( ) | Read ( ) <br> ReadObjectInfo ( ) <br> Compare ( ) |
| Search operations | Search ( ) <br> List ( ) | Search ( ) <br> List ( ) |
| Modify operations | AddEntry ( ) <br><br> RemoveEntry ( ) <br><br> ModifyEntry ( ) <br> ModifyRDN ( ) | AddObject ( ) <br><br> RemoveObject ( ) <br><br> ModifyObject ( ) <br> ModifyRDN ( ) |

**Figure 12.5** The mapping of XDS and NDS function calls.

Figure 12.6 shows how applications written to the NDS API could also easily talk to a fully compliant X.500 directory service through the addition of a function translation layer. This means that developers can write to the XDS API and map applications transparently to NDS and vice versa. Applications designed to interface to NDS could be easily adapted to run on an X.500 server which uses the XDS interface.

## 12.5 DEPLOYMENT OF X.500 BY PUBLIC SERVICE PROVIDERS

X.500 was largely designed to meet the business requirements of public service providers in enhancing their information services. Currently, the majority of public service directory services are tied to a specific electronic mail service. The main purpose of the directory service is to find the electronic mail address of subscribers within the service. Access to directory information is limited to other subscribers of the service. For example, MCI Mail's directory service can be accessed only by MCI Mail subscribers, and AT&T's directory service can be accessed only by AT&T Mail subscribers.

Typically, the information that is housed in the directory is limited to the electronic mail address, the physical location of the individual (usually city and state), and the organization and department to which he or she is affiliated.

Some public directory services provide the ability to limit access to within a par-

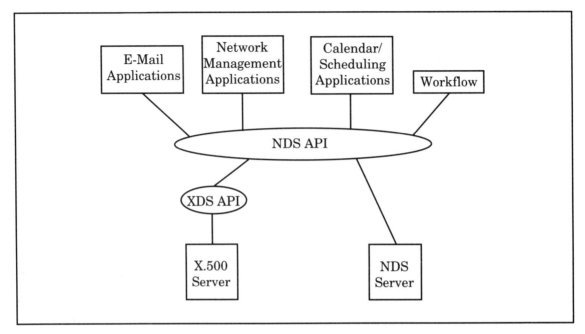

**Figure 12.6** NDS-to-XDS API mapping.

ticular subscriber base. For instance, both GE Information Services and AT&T Easylink will allow a corporation to have a closed user group. This means that only the people who are listed in the user group will have access to that user group's directory information. Being a member of the closed user group does not inhibit access to the open or public directory or the sending of mail to other subscribers outside the group.

### 12.5.1 X.500 Deployment

Public service providers are working on the development of commercial X.500 services. X.500 is intended to provide the basis for interconnecting public providers to create a single, worldwide information base that will facilitate the ability to find and access information. Consequently, a whole new class of value-added services including worldwide access, directory lookup, synchronization, and remote access are likely to emerge based on the use of X.500 technology.

It is important to note, however, that the deployment of directory services within public data networks presents a number of special issues, particularly in the areas of security and privacy. For instance, the directory information that public carriers will store is bounded by what individuals and corporations are willing to provide and to whom they are willing to give access. Since X.500 directories contain listings for people, objects, and extensive attributes, public service providers are in a very sensitive position with respect to information about individuals, fax machines, printers, servers, and other devices and objects.

### 12.5.2 Directory Lookup

The first implementations of X.500 will supply directory lookup, which allows users to query for directory information on any individual independent of the public or private e-mail system in use. This is very similar to what is available today, with the addition that the query is not bound to only one public service provider, but can be checked against any interconnected directory service. For example, if you are looking for the electronic mail address of John Smith at Widget Manufacturing, you would send a query to your public service provider. If your public service provider is unable to find this listing in its directory, it would pass the request to other public service providers worldwide to see if John Smith were listed with them. While this is the most commonly envisioned application of public directory services, it is also one of the most difficult to successfully implement for the following reasons:

1. It is difficult to ensure the technical integrity of the information across large networks—potentially thousands—of DSAs.
2. The nature of the business relationship between service providers. One issue, for instance, is how to charge for queries that involve cooperation among several service providers.
3. The competitive pressure among different service providers makes cooperation difficult.

### 12.5.3 Directory Synchronization and Remote Access

Public services will also offer directory synchronization services. Companies will be able to upload their directories from multiple locations and from multiple messaging platforms to the public service provider, which will then perform the necessary translation (such as converting cc:Mail to an X.400 or NetWare MHS format) and download the information back to the various internal directories. This information would also be accessible to remote users who find it impractical to store the entire corporate directory local.

### 12.5.4 Trading Community Directory Services

A trading community may be comprised of an industry segment (e.g. the Aerospace industry) or a corporation's vendors, suppliers, and customers. These trading communities have a great need to communicate with one another about purchase orders, arranging meetings, quotations on bids, and other business transactions. Through the services of public providers, trading communities can control the types of information shared among their constituents.

### 12.5.5 Accessing Public Directory Services

Public service providers will provide access in much the same way that they provide access today. A user will access the X.500 directory online or through a store-and-forward mechanism. With the continued proliferation of LAN-based e-mail systems, many directory queries will be initiated using store and forward technology. A query from these platforms means that the user is not initiating the connection to the directory service; rather, a gateway on his or her e-mail system is initiating the connection.

### 12.5.6 Obstacles to the Realization of Worldwide Directory Services

A variety of competitive, business, and technical obstacles are retarding the deployment of X.500 by public service providers. The major factors include:

- The nature of X.500 and the number of technical issues involved requires that public service providers work together to deliver global directory services. In particular, the implementation of a worldwide X.500 directory service requires a level of cooperation far greater than what was necessary to implement X.400 e-mail interconnections, where messages are passed, but access is not required to a common source of information.
- Many corporations have multiple e-mail systems and are struggling with the issue of directory synchronization. Many of the products that are being implemented by corporations to tackle this problem are proprietary in nature. As more and more proprietary systems are implemented, the difficulty of hooking these systems into a public carrier may slow the "pure" realization of X.500.
- As with any standard, there is room for different interpretations by different implementors. The public service providers will have to work through these different implementations and reconcile the areas that have been interpreted differently.
- Common naming and registration procedures must be defined and adhered to. Registration and knowledge issues are critical because, although the design of directory information tree is worked out well in the standards, there are problems with implementing the model in a commercial environment. For example, if one X.500 service provider furnishes the Widget Corporation's internal electronic mail user listings and another furnishes its telephone directory listing, the providers might list some entries twice with only partial and possibly conflicting information. Without common naming and registration procedures, a user may be given partial and possibly conflicting information from two public providers.

The U.S. public service providers are active in pursuing X.500. Many of these providers have joined to create the North American Directory Forum (see Appendix B), which is working on the deployment of an experimental directory service pilot.

The service providers are all in varying stages of their X.500 implementations. Carriers like GE, AT&T, BT Tymnet, and Pac Bell have publicly stated their intention to support and develop an X.500 service. Because the public service providers are in very different stages of development and deployment, and the

X.500 standard is still evolving (as evidenced by the 1993 extensions), the realization of X.500-based directory public service interconnections is still several years away.

### 12.5.7 Pricing Issues

An issue of particular complexity for public service providers is how to charge for directory services. Today, there is usually no direct cost associated with a directory search; the prevailing view has been that for every directory search that is initiated, a revenue-generating message will be created and sent. However, this is likely to change in the near future. A new pricing model will be required for directory services to pay for the value-added services that providers are supplying. These additional services incur additional costs for several reasons:

- The information that is housed in the directory will expand significantly to include not only user names and e-mail addresses, but a variety of other corporate and network information.
- Public service providers will supply additional services beyond simple lookup capabilities, for which they will charge.
- The interconnection of public services necessitates settlement of charges between service providers.

Public provxiders are likely to rely on a variety of pricing models due to the different types of information that can be stored and the different types of services that may be offered. Prices may be based on the number of transactions, the amount of data stored, a flat fee, or a combination of these.

Some of the factors that will be used to determine price include:

- Apportioning charges among different public service providers.
- Data storage costs.
- System costs for conducting a search or updating the database.
- Costs associated with delivering the information to the requester.
- Types of information requested; the provider may charge different rates for different types of requested information.

# 13

## Application Programming Interfaces

Standard, "open" APIs (those that are published and publicly available) are particularly important in the area of directory services because they define the boundary between the directory service and applications that rely on directory information. Consequently, the establishment of an industry-standard API affects the widespread commercial deployment of directory service technology.

The availability of a standard, published API is perhaps more important with directory services than with any other network component because directory services are really only useful if they can be accessed, queried, and modified by a wide range of different distributed applications. When an open standard API is available, information stored in the directory database can be used by applications provided by any vendor or third-party developer, as well as by custom applications developed by end-users themselves. This chapter examines several leading industry standard APIs for directory services, including open directory service (XDS), vendor independent messaging (VIM), Microsoft's messaging application programming interface (MAPI).

The XDS API is the only directory-services API that has a formal status as a standard, having been developed by a consortium of vendors (X/Open and the XAPI Association—see Appendix B) and ratified by POSIX as a standard interface for UNIX systems. VIM and MAPI represent efforts currently underway by some of the major vendors in the PC LAN industry to define a set of open programming interfaces for messaging and directory services. While VIM and MAPI are intended primarily as APIs for messaging applications, both also provide extensive facilities for querying and managing address books and directories.

## 13.1 DIRECTORY APPLICATION PROGRAMMING INTERFACES

Unlike a protocol, which defines the format of data transferred between two machines over a network connection, an API defines the internal interface between different layers of code providing differing levels of functionality. Figure 13.1 shows the architectural role of a generic API.

The availability of an industry-standard API at the boundary between applications and network services—that is, for directories, messaging store-and-forward engines, and so forth—opens up the possibility of mixing and matching applications and back-end network services from various vendors. This in turn provides several important advantages.

1. Applications can be developed separately from the underlying engine. This means that the engine and the applications can evolve independently of each other, provided that the interface through which they communicate remains the same. Where the interface needs to change to better reflect new back-end functionality, the changes can be made available at the API level to a whole range of applications in a well-controlled manner.

2. Application developers need only be familiar with the API, not with the engine internals. This makes it possible for application developers to write applications (such as e-mail front-ends) without having to first become experts in how the underlying directory functionality is implemented. All they need to understand is the behavior of the API.

3. Applications can be readily developed by third parties. Provided the API is well-defined, well-documented, and available in the public domain, practically anyone can write to it. This means that over time,

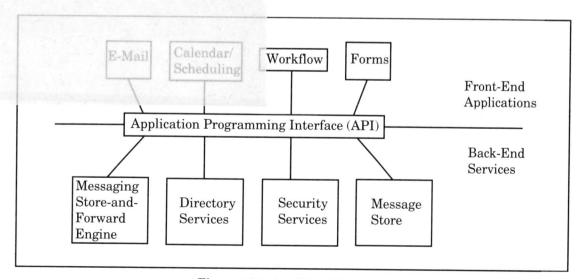

**Figure 13.1** An API architecture.

more applications are likely to emerge to provide a range of functionality and creativity that could not be achieved through the efforts of a single vendor.

## 13.2 XDS

The XDS API was developed by the X.400 API Association in conjunction with X/Open, a consortium of UNIX vendors. XDS is the programmatic interface to an X.500 directory system agent (DSA). It is designed to be used in conjunction with the XOM (X.400 association object management) API, which provides a generic set of function calls for managing data structures. The XOM API was designed originally in support of the X.400 API Association's messaging APIs. It was considered useful to rely on a common set of object management function calls to manage both X.400 message objects and X.500 directory entries. Figure 13.2 illustrates how the XDS and XOM APIs would be deployed within a directory client and server environment.

XDS is the most common standard interface to X.500-based directories in use today. It was adopted by OSF/DCE (see Appendix B) as part of its set of standard interface specifications, and has been successfully approved within POSIX as the standard interface of UNIX-based X.500 directory implementations.

From a technical standpoint, XDS closely resembles the X.500 DAP protocol, providing all the same function calls, arguments, and result structures. It adds the ability for function calls to be treated either synchronously (where the client waits until the procedure completes and returns before going on to other tasks) as specified in X.500, or asynchronously (where the client is able to process other

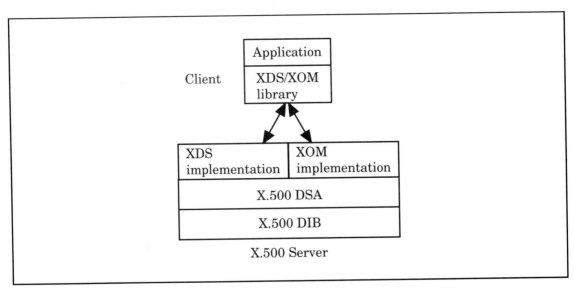

**Figure 13.2** XDS/XOM architecture.

tasks and is notified by the interface when the procedure has completed). The asynchronous style of operation is not part of the X.500 standards, but was overwhelmingly requested by product implementors to provide more flexibility and better performance in multitasking environments.

The XDS API has been criticized for its reliance on the XOM object management API, which most developers in the industry consider unnecessarily complex, difficult to use, and costly in terms of performance. This has led some vendors (such as Hewlett-Packard) to deploy their own higher-level APIs on top of XDS/XOM, to make programming to standard X.500 directory services easier to independent software vendors (ISVs). The introduction of a standard, simpler API for use in conjunction with XDS would help to promote wider deployment of X.500 directory services by making the technology more accessible to nonspecialists.

## 13.3 VIM

Vendor-independent messaging (VIM) was developed by a consortium of vendors consisting of Lotus, Novell, Borland, and Apple. IBM has also endorsed VIM technology, due to its close relationships with Lotus and Apple. VIM is designed as a comprehensive API for open messaging, which provides extensive support for messaging, directories, message stores, authentication and security. Figure 13.3 shows the VIM architecture. From an architectural standpoint, VIM is similar to XDS in that it standardizes the interface between applications and back-end services. In order to achieve application portability, however, VIM needs to be implemented across a wide range of back-end network services.

VIM relies on the use of distinguished names to uniquely name recipients across all the address books to which the VIM implementation has access. Address books

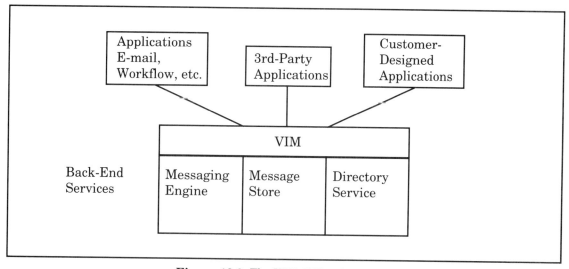

**Figure 13.3** The VIM API architecture.

are databases of named entries, typically representing messaging recipients. VIM is designed to support messaging systems with multiple address books. Address books usually consist of a personal address book and one or more public address books. In the VIM abstraction, an address book entry is a database record consisting of a unique name, a type, and a set of attributes. VIM defines two kinds of entries that model either persons, which represent mailboxes associated with end-users, or groups, which represent lists of persons or other group names. Nested groups are also supported. VIM identifies two ways to specify a message recipient: direct and indirect. *Direct addresses* consist of the name of the target system (which is also the pathname of the entity's distinguished name), the name of the entity, and the type of the recipient of the message (that is, a user, a group, a printer, and so on). It also includes a native name, which is messaging-system specific (an SMTP name or an X.400 name, for instance). Inclusion of native names allows preexisting addressing formats to be embedded and carried along within a VIM address.

*Indirect addresses,* on the other hand, are address book entries that must be queried to obtain their distinguished name. The indirect addresses consist of the name of an address book—which contains the recipient's entry, the name of the recipient, the type of recipient (either a group or a user)—and, optionally, a native name.

## 13.4 MAPI

Microsoft's Windows Open Service Architecture (WOSA) defines a set of APIs designed to insulate applications from the specifics of network service implementations. MAPI is the messaging component of WOSA. It allows mail-enabled applications to transparently access the services provided by multiple network services.

Unlike XDS and VIM, MAPI offers a dual interface structure. Figure 13.4 shows the MAPI architecture. Applications see a client API that provides facilities to read, send mail, and manage address book entries. Back-end service providers (such as directory mail services, transport services, security services, and so forth) see a set of service provider interfaces (SPIs) that permit these services to "plug into" the MAPI client interface through a service provider driver at the workstation. As a result, no changes are required to the service providers in order to support MAPI-compliant applications.

Microsoft has designed two application interfaces for MAPI: Simple MAPI and Power MAPI. Simple MAPI is a subset of the full MAPI functionality, and provides a set of simple procedures for reading and sending mail messages, including documents and attachments. Power MAPI is a more sophisticated interface that includes address books and message stores, as well as facilities to manage very large attachments of information.

One of the major advantages of MAPI is that its dual set of application and service-provider interfaces makes it possible for client applications to become truly independent from the implementation details of the back-end service implemen-

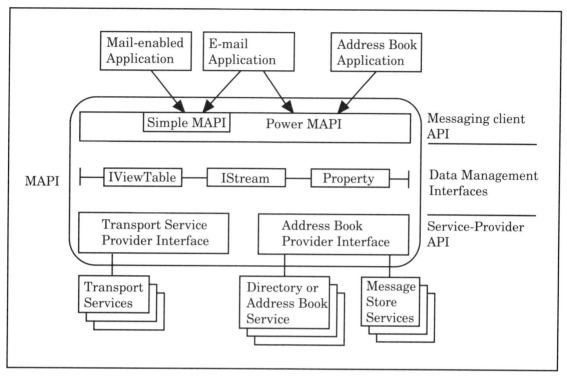

**Figure 13.4** The MAPI architecture.

tations. This simplifies application migration, since no changes to back-end net-work servers are required in order to support MAPI. In the case of VIM and XDS, application independence can be achieved only if every back-end service provider supports the same API (either VIM or XDS) as the back-end API.

The potential downside to MAPI, however, is that it may lead to some loss of functionality to those applications where the back-end service model differs con-siderably from the model of data structures and function calls expected by the MAPI SPIs. In effect, applications are trading off full access to the back-end server functionality in exchange for increased portability.

MAPI address books are made up of *containers,* which are folders. Each con-tainer consists of at least one list of recipients, and each list is itself a container. An address book may be laid out as a single container, a flat list of containers, or a hierarchy of containers. This allows MAPI to be overlaid on top of a large num-ber of directory service providers. The contents of address books are viewed through the use of table operations. Regardless of the number of directory service providers installed, applications see only one address book. The personal address book im-plementation provided by MAPI will generally contain copies of the entries stored in the system-level directory provider. This form of local caching helps to reduce the frequency of directory queries for frequently used recipient information.

# 14

## Directory Synchronization

---

This chapter looks into the more prevalent techniques available to support the integration of heterogeneous directory services, also known as directory synchronization. Directory synchronization has emerged as one of the critical needs of large enterprise networks. While most organizations have successfully tied together their e-mail systems through gateways or some kind of backbone integration approach, the problem that remains is how to integrate the naming and addressing information stored in the diverse proprietary directories associated with each different e-mail system.

### 14.1 THE GOALS BEHIND DIRECTORY SYNCHRONIZATION

Directory services integration represents one of the major obstacles to full network integration for organizations with disparate network architectures that are rightsizing their computing environments. In particular, these organizations are struggling with how to provide users (and applications) throughout the network with access to all the other users and resources, even those that are registered on different directory services throughout the network. In addition, many organizations are seeking to consolidate information currently spread across multiple different directory services and address books into a single, unified corporate directory database. Such a corporate directory (sometimes referred to as the *global directory*) is considered essential to the effective management and administration of user information in large organizations.

Directory synchronization is intended to address these requirements by performing several important functions, including:

1. Providing a central repository for all network naming and addressing information,
2. Ensuring that information updates are communicated between the central directory repository and the local heterogeneous directory environments, and finally,
3. Providing visibility of all network names and addresses to users in each of the native environments.

## 14.2 DIRECTORY GATEWAYS

Gateways are still the most commonly used approach for directory integration. They use specialized agents that reside within the directory server in order to send or gather updates from foreign directory servers. SoftSwitch, for example, provides a wide range of directory synchronization agents that allow its integration product to consolidate various naming and addressing information from multiple directory services. Likewise, companies such as Lotus/cc:Mail and Microsoft offer tools for importing and exporting information between directory services and external environments such as PROFS and SMTP. A number of message integration products integrate directory information from multiple sources into a central database structure.

The emergence of industry standard APIs will make it easier for vendors to design directory synchronization solutions by opening up the interface to a range of native address books and directory services.

## 14.3 A DIRECTORY SYNCHRONIZATION ARCHITECTURE

Directory synchronization products typically rely on a server/agent architecture to automatically propagate directory information across a heterogeneous e-mail network. A specialized protocol (often simply implemented in terms of e-mail messages) is used to send update information between the server and the agents. Three main components typically make up a directory synchronization solution:

- A directory server.
- Agents for each e-mail environment (or address book) to which integration is desired.
- A protocol that supports the exchange of information between the server and the agents.

The server provides a central repository for all naming and addressing information to a number of attached agents. Each agent sends information about its users to the server and updates its local directory (or address book) with information it obtains from the server. The result is that the server and all the agents

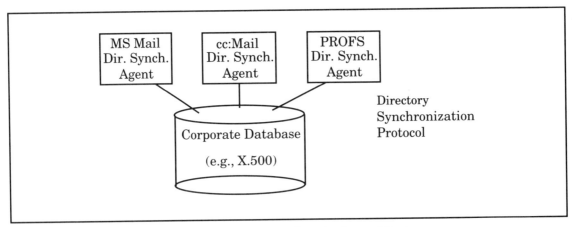

**Figure 14.1**  Directory synchronization architecture.

have copies of the global naming information for the network. Figure 14.1 illustrates such an architecture.

### 14.3.1 The Directory Server

The directory server maintains all addresses in a master directory database. The server receives changes from the agents and, on a scheduled basis, propagates these changes to all the other agents. On-demand updates are typically also available (that is, the agent requests to download update information from the master).

The directory server may be implemented using any kind of centralized or distributed database, ranging from a simple flat file to a relational database. Increasingly, corporate users are looking to X.500 to provide the directory server database. The main reason for this is that X.500 is inherently a distributed and replicated database. Also, X.500 provides a standard naming structure that can serve as a common naming structure across a variety of heterogeneous naming schemes.

### 14.3.2 The Agents

The agents monitor the local e-mail systems for directory changes. On a scheduled basis, each agent converts the changes to an agreed-upon name format, and sends the changes to the directory server. Upon receiving all changes from the server, each agent converts the changes to its native format and updates its local e-mail directory or address book. The result is that all e-mail end-users have transparent access to all e-mail addresses.

Each agent understands the local directory or address book environment, and supports some form of name conversion scheme that allows all addresses propagated from the server to be rendered to the local e-mail user in their native format.

### 14.3.3 The Protocol

The protocol for directory synchronization is typically based on e-mail messages. That is, there is an assumption that an e-mail transport mechanism is already in place (for example, X.400, STMP, SNADS). The update information exchanged is encoded as the data portion of e-mail messages that are exchanged between the directory synchronization server and its agents.

## 14.4 DIRECTORY EXCHANGE (DX)

The Directory Exchange (DX), originally developed by Retix, is one of the first attempts to standardize a directory synchronization architecture. DX defines an X.400 e-mail–based protocol for sending update information among different directory services, and was specifically designed to integrate proprietary LAN directory environments into an X.400/X.500 e-mail backbone infrastructure.

DX is based on a client/server model comprising a DX agent (DXA) and a DX server (DXS). The DX agent is coresident with an e-mail gateway, and is responsible for extracting user information from its associated e-mail system. It then conveys the information to a DX server, which consolidates it into a centralized directory database. DX agents and DX servers interact by means of X.400 e-mail messages. A specialized protocol is defined to strictly define the format and content of the X.400 e-mail messages exchanged between DX agents and servers. Figure 14.2 summarizes the main components that make up the DX architecture.

Figure 14.3 shows the architecture of a network environment that utilizes the DX technology to perform directory synchronization. The communication between

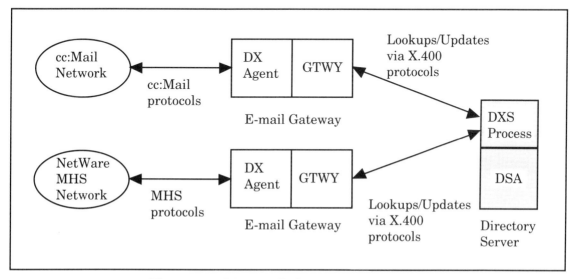

**Figure 14.2** Directory Exchange (DX) architecture.

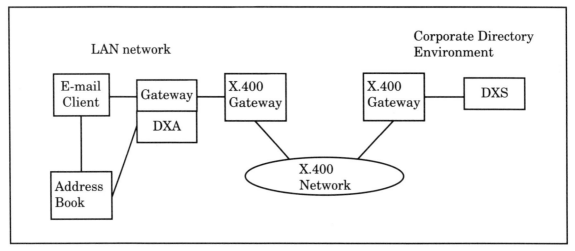

**Figure 14.3** Directory Exchange (DX) network configuration.

the DX agent and the DX server must occur over an X.400 e-mail network. Note that the DXS could be implemented either as an X.500 directory service or as another kind of data repository (a relational database, a flat file, and so forth).

### 14.4.1 The DX Protocol

The DX specification defines the protocol format in which the DX agents send information to the DX server. The DX design assumes that the X.400 protocol is being used to exchange information between DX agents and DX servers. The DX server therefore must reside on a server that is able to receive X.400 messages. X.400 over OSI and X.400 over TCP/IP stacks are permitted. The DX server must also be able to parse the contents of the message according to the format defined by the DX specification in order to obtain the required naming information to be added to and removed from the central directory database.

### 14.4.2 An Evaluation of DX

From an architectural standpoint, DX is one of the more advanced models of directory integration available in the public domain. It is flexible, yet simple to understand, which makes it straightforward to implement on a wide range of platform types. It provides a very powerful model with support for a variety of topologies to best meet diverse interconnection and administrative requirements. One of the major contributions of DX is that it proves that the directory services integration can be successfully addressed. Since the DX specification is in the public domain, we can expect that it will serve as a framework and catalyst for e-mail vendors to do further work this area.

The main drawback to the widespread commercial use of DX as it is currently defined is that it assumes an X.400 message handling network infrastructure. The

DX protocol is specified entirely in the context of X.400 mail messages, and cannot be used with other e-mail transport without being redesigned. X.400 is gaining in popularity, but still represents a very small fraction of the e-mail market. Users who do not have an X.400 network in place or do not plan to move to X.400 in the near future have no way to deploy DX. While DX provides many valuable advantages in terms of directory integration, it is unlikely that users would be able to justify the costs of migrating to X.400 solely on the basis of DX.

Nevertheless, in environments that have already adopted an X.400/X.500 backbone messaging infrastructure, DX provides an excellent standard mechanism for integrating PC LAN and other proprietary e-mail networks into the network. It can also be expected that over time the DX architecture will be adapted to operate over a wider range of e-mail transports besides X.400 (such as SMTP and Netware MHS). One such example is SDX (developed by Hitachi), which defines a DX-like protocol over SMTP.

## 14.5 THE OSF/DCE MODEL

The Open Standards Foundation/Distributed Computing Architecture (OSF/DCE) is a set of standards and implementations agreed upon by a consortium of leading UNIX vendors. OSF/DCE has formulated an architecture for directory integration that can also serve as a model for directory integration.

The OSF/DCE architecture, shown in Figure 14.4, consists of cell directories deployed at the local level, either within a single LAN segment or a collection of LANs that form a single administrative workgroup environment, and a global directory service that provides an integration point for information from across all cell directories. Understanding that internetworks can be both very large and widely distributed geographically, the OSF architecture assumes that both cell directories and global directories will consist of distributed and replicated services.

A component called a *global directory agent* (GDA) allows cell directories to exchange data with the global directory. The GDA acts as a mechanism to forward queries that cannot be successfully resolved within the cell directory environment to the global directory for resolution. The global directory must have sufficient knowledge of the layout of the network to forward the queries to another cell directory in a completely different part of the network if necessary.

The OSF/DCE model differs from the directory synchronization architectures described earlier for two reasons. First, the GDA is an active component that receives a query from a cell directory and reformats it as a native query to the global directory service. That is, it addresses the need for goal 3 as described in Section 14.1.

Second, it seeks to solve only the issue of how to exchange queries between dissimilar directory services rather than addressing the need to maintain a complete copy of all network naming and addressing with a central corporate directory. It does not, therefore, attempt to satisfy goals 1 and 2 in Section 14.1

Regardless of whether OSF/DCE becomes a leading technology in the marketplace, OSF's directory services model represents an accepted strategy for inte-

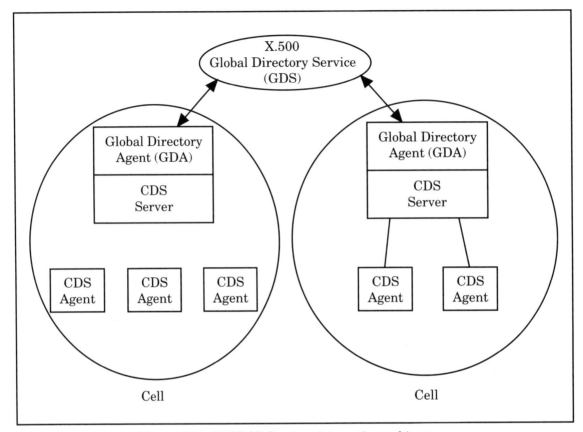

**Figure 14.4**  OSF/DCE directory integration architecture.

grating heterogeneous directory services. Even vendors that are not associated with OSF are adopting a similar architectural model to explain how their non-X.500 based directory service implementations can coexist and interoperate with X.500 directory services. For instance, vendors of PC LAN directory products find it straightforward to view their non-X.500 products as "cell" directories that interact with corporate-level X.500 directory services through a specialized directory agent (which is in effect a gateway from their own implementation to X.500). Nevertheless, OSF/DCE is primarily a model for gateway-based integration. A great deal of definition work still remains to specify how all the components of the OSF/DCE directory environment will interact with each other. Furthermore, users wishing to use the OSF technology for directory services can do so only by adopting OSF's entire suite of UNIX-based protocols and applications.

# APPENDIX A: STANDARDS REFERENCE DOCUMENTS

## A.1 THE 1988 X.500 RECOMMENDATIONS

The set of documents that make up the 1988 X.500 standards are listed below.

| Title | CCITT | ISO |
|---|---|---|
| *The Directory: Overview of Concepts, Models and Services* | X.500 | 9594-1 |
| *The Directory: Models* Describes the principles of operation and provides the overall service description for the X.500 standards | X.501 | 9594-2 |
| *The Directory: Authentication Framework* Defines a set of simple and strong authentication techniques, including the use of certificates and digital signatures. | X.509 | 9594.8 |
| *The Directory: Abstract Service Definition* Service description from the point of view of the directory user. | X.511 | 9594-3 |
| *The Directory: Distributed Operations* Defines the distribute behavior of the directory service, including knowledge and name resolution. | X.518 | 9594-4 |
| *The Directory: Protocol Specifications* DAP and DSP protocol definition, mapping onto the lower-layer services. | X.519 | 9594-5 |

| | | |
|---|---|---|
| *The Directory: Selected Attribute Types* | X.520 | 9594-6 |
| Internationally standardized attributes. | | |
| *The Directory: Selected Object Classes* | X.521 | 9594-7 |
| Internationally standardized classes. | | |

## A.2 SUPPORTING STANDARDS

In addition, X.500 relies on the OSI standards and specifications listed below.

| *Standard* | *CCITT* | *ISO* |
|---|---|---|
| OSI: Basic Reference Model | X.200 | 7498 |
| OSI: Specification of Abstract Syntax Notation One (ASN.1) | X.208 | 8824 |
| OSI: Specification of Basic Encoding Rules for Abstract Syntax Notation One (ASN.1) | X.209 | 8825 |
| OSI: Association Control: Service Definition | X.217 | 8649 |
| OSI: Reliable Transfer: Model and Service Definition | X.218 | 9066-1 |
| OSI: Remote Operations: Model, Notation, and Service Definition | X.219 | 9072-1 |
| OSI: Association Control: Protocol Specification | X.227 | 8650 |
| OSI: Reliable Transfer: Protocol Specification | X.228 | 9066-2 |
| OSI: Remote Operations: Protocol Specification | X.229 | 9072-2 |

## A.3 THE 1993 X.500 RECOMMENDATIONS

The 1993 edition of the X.500 standards includes one new recommendation (X.525, on replication) and revised text for most of the existing 1988 documents. Note that the revised documents maintain the same CCITT/ISO numbers but are identifiable by a 1993 date of publication.

| | *CCITT* | *ISO* |
|---|---|---|
| The Directory: Overview of Concepts, Models and Services (1993) | X.500 | 9594-1 |
| The Directory: Models (1993) | X.501 | 9594-2 |
| The Directory: Authentication Framework (1993) | X.509 | 9594-8 |
| The Directory: Abstract Service Definition (1993) | X.511 | 9594-3 |
| The Directory: Models (1993) | X.518 | 9594-4 |

The Directory: Protocol Specifications (1993)    X.519    9594-5
The Directory: Selected Attribute Types (1993)    X.520    9594-6
The Directory: Selected Object Classes (1993)    X.521    9594-7
The Directory: Replication (1993)    X.525    9594-9

# APPENDIX B: STANDARDS AND CONSORTIUMS

A variety of official standards bodies and consortiums have been formed to develop standards, implementation frameworks, and conformance testing. Formal standards bodies such as the International Organization for Standardization (ISO) and the Consultative Committee for International Telephony and Telegraphy (CCITT) have developed a number of protocols for Open Systems Interconnection (OSI) over the past decade, including X.400 and X.500. As *de jure* standards, these have a legal value beyond simply that they are published specifications. In particular, they can be officially referenced by government procurement guidelines.

The specification of international standards by ISO and CCITT represents only the first step in the commercial deployment of the technology. Because international standards strive to remain independent of the actual implementation details, other committees, called *functional standards groups,* are often involved in defining additional rules and agreements describing finer details of how the international standards are actually to be implemented and tested. The activity carried out by these groups is called *profiling,* and deals more closely with specifying any aspect of interoperability that may have been left open to choice in the international standards.

The National Institute for Standards and Technology (NIST) in the United States is a functional standards group. NIST hosts a series of workshops for implementors called the OSI Implementor's Workshops (OIW) for the purpose of defining the pragmatic rules to which implementors must adhere when developing OSI systems. NIST publishes a new set of documents each year, called the Implementors Agreements. These agreements are used by computer vendors as a detailed guide on how to implement the OSI standards, including the X.500 product offerings.

Counterparts to NIST exist in Europe and the Pacific Rim. The principal organization in Europe is called the European Workshop for Open Systems (EWOS). EWOS has a legal status within the European Economic Community (EEC). In Japan, the functional standards group is the Interoperability Technology Association for Information Processing (INTAP).

The NIST Implementor's Agreements and the functional profiles published by the other regional standards organizations form the technical basis for the specification of Government Open Systems Interconnection Profiles (GOSIP). GOSIP specifications are procurement guidelines published by national governments to guide the procurement of computer equipment by their government agencies.

GOSIP specifications have been published by the U.S. government, the U.K. government, and many other governments throughout the world. They are driving demand for X.500 directory services in governmental sectors.

Organizations such as COS, X/Open, and the XAPIA are consortiums of vendors and users that focus on particular technical or implementation issues of the standards. These bodies contribute significantly to the deployment of standards by developing implementation tools, technologies, and test suites to ensure compatibility between vendor implementations.

## B.1 ISO AND CCITT

X.500 was developed in close cooperation between ISO and CCITT. ISO is a voluntary organization made up of the standards defining bodies of most of the industrialized nations of the world (e.g. ANSI, BSI, etc). Work in ISO's technical committees is carried out primarily by technical representatives from the leading computer vendors, in conjunction with academic researchers. ISO has played a leading role over the past two decades in the development of the OSI architecture.

CCITT, on the other hand, is a treaty organization set up by agreement among national governments. It operates under the auspices of the United Nations as part of the International Telecommunication Union (ITU). CCITT defines the standards and procedures that must be followed by all national Postal, Telegraph, and Telephone (PTT) administrations when interconnecting for the purposes of providing telephone and telecommunication services on a worldwide basis. Members of CCITT comprise all the national PTTs, including privately owned service providers such as AT&T and MCI.

ISO and CCITT are beginning to cooperate more closely on all aspects of OSI standardization, with the ultimate goal of achieving closer interoperability between the networking services offered by public service providers and those provided by computer vendors. Much of the design of the X.500 standards for directory services reflects input from CCITT in support of the business and strategic requirements of public service providers.

## B.2 GOSIP

The Government Open Systems Interconnection Profile (GOSIP) is a set of communication and networking specifications based on the OSI architecture, for use by government agencies in the procurement of information systems equipment. Where OSI is a broad architecture based on a set of international standards for data communications, GOSIP specifications represent a refinement, or subset, of the OSI architecture to fit the specific needs of the government user community. In developing GOSIP specifications, governments generally aim to:

1. Facilitate the procurement and acceptance testing of communications-based products.
2. Ensure that different and separately procured departmental systems can interwork to an assured level of functionality.
3. Provide a clear specification to manufacturers on which to base product development.

GOSIP specifications have been published in the United States, the United Kingdom, a number of European nations, Japan, and Australia. In addition, organizations such as NATO and the EEC are also developing procurement guidelines based on the OSI architecture. Generally, GOSIP specifications are based on the profiling work of functional standards groups such as NIST in the United States, and CEN/CENELEC and CEPT in Europe. Though in the longterm it is likely that a number of these GOSIP specifications will be fully aligned with one another, particularly in the United States and Europe, differences will continue to exist over the next few years.

Most governments that have published GOSIP specifications are making compliance with GOSIP mandatory for all government procurement. This means that in those product areas where a GOSIP requirement exists (such as e-mail), vendors must be able to show a GOSIP-compliant product in order to be included in the procurement cycle. In addition, the government procurement process will include a careful scrutiny of the vendor's strategic direction toward a full line of OSI- and GOSIP-compliant products. To date, most GOSIP specifications worldwide have not made X.500 a mandatory component of their OSI requirements. This was largely due to the lack of access controls and replication in the 1988 version of the standards. With the publication of 1993 X.500, this is likely to change very rapidly, and most government GOSIP specifications are expected to mandate use of X.500 directory services by the end of 1993. They are generally expected to require adherence to 1988 X.500 and support of the 1993 access controls; they are not likely to mandate full support of 1993 X.500 functionality.

## B.3 OSINET

OSINet is a network of vendors set up to test interoperability among OSI implementations. In the United States, OSINet has sprung up out of the activities of NIST, whereas in Europe a similar organization called EUROSINet has emerged within EWOS. OSINet provides extensive test suites to test interoperability between implementations. Companies and research organizations participating in OSINet register their availability as a testing partner and make available a dedicated machine that can be contacted via dial-up X.25 connections at any time by any of the other OSINet participants. The list of available test partners and their network access information is then published on a regular basis and distributed to all participants. Any company wishing to test its implementation simply schedules connect time with one or more partners and runs the OSINet test suites. The greater number of partners an implementation tests with successfully, the more likely it is that it adequately conforms to the protocol standard specifications.

## B.4 COS

The Corporation for Open Systems (COS) is a consortium of vendors formed in the late 1980s to implement a framework for conformance testing of OSI products. The goal of the consortium is to develop the necessary tools and technologies to ensure that vendors that manufacture OSI products do, in fact, implement the protocols as defined by the international standards. In order to satisfy this goal, COS develops test scripts and selects *reference implementations.* The assumption is that if two products test successfully against a reference implementation, they will also be able to interoperate correctly. A set of test scripts are provided by COS to ensure that each vendor's product passes a common set of tests before being certified as meeting conformance. Products that meet conformance requirements are issued a COS mark, which indicates that the product has successfully passed all the required conformance tests.

To date, COS has developed mark programs for FTAM (File Transfer Access and Management), OSI lower-layer components, and X.400. The mark program for X.500 directory services has been slow in developing and is not widely used by vendors. One of the reasons for the slow progress of X.500 conformance tests is the level of complexity of the standard itself. Clearly, the X.500 standards present a much richer set of features and functionality than traditional communication protocols. This presents a real challenge in terms of defining the appropriate behavior of the system in response to various predefined queries.

Overall, the COS program has also not been successful, largely because the idea of testing against a reference implementation has proved less effective than interoperability testing. The complexity of OSI application-layer standards, such as X.500, is such that passing conformance tests against a reference implementation does not in itself guarantee that two products will interwork with each other. Additional work is required to ensure full interoperability between the products themselves in a real deployment scenario.

Vendors have found it more useful to simply perform interoperability testing among themselves, and to assume that if their product is able to interwork successfully with those of one or more other vendors, then it is ready for commercial release. Clearly, the larger the number of vendors tested against, the greater the probability that all potential interoperability defects have been sorted out prior to product release. Over the past couple years, most vendors have shifted their testing efforts to interoperability testing groups such as OSINet (managed by NIST) in the United States and EUROSINet in Europe.

Vendors of X.500 products today typically claim conformance to the standard based on their participation in either OSINet or EUROSINet interoperability testing programs, on adherence to functional profiles such as NIST or EWOS, or both.

## B.5 X.400 API ASSOCIATION

The popularity of X.400 as an electronic mail interchange standard has led to the development of a set of standard application programming interfaces (APIs) for X.400 products. In 1988 a group of North American vendors and service suppliers formed an organization called the X.400 API Association. The association's goal was to develop and publish a set of standard interfaces for X.400 software products, to enable vendors and service suppliers to mix-and-match within their own products X.400 software components developed by other suppliers.

In 1989, the X.400 API Association merged its efforts with those of another standards group called X/Open. X/Open is an international consortium of vendors, including many U.S. vendors, that have long been developing standards to cover major aspects of applications portability in UNIX-based computing environments. Together, the X.400 API Association and X/Open embarked on the development of a set of X.500 directory services APIs called XDS (X/Open Directory Service APIs). XDS consists of a directory service API that closely mirrors the X.500 DAP functionality and an object management API called XOM (X/Open Object Management API), which is also part of the suite of the X.400 suite of APIs.

## B.6 X/OPEN

X/Open is a consortium of UNIX vendors who develop standards and approve a common set of technologies for inclusion within UNIX operating environments. X/Open collaborated extensively with the X.400 API Association in the development of the X.500 directory service APIs, called XDS (X/Open Directory Services). The XDS API has become the leading industry standard API used in most commercial X.500 product implementations.

## B.7 NADF

The North American Directory Forum (NADF) is a consortium of public service providers that have come together to develop a framework for the commercial deployment of public data network directory services based on the X.500 standards. Members of the NADF include companies such as AT&T, Sprint, and BNR. While most of the members of the NADF are North American public service providers, a number of European service providers have also become involved. NADF's mission is to develop a single public directory for North America that includes all North American public e-mail providers.

NADF's work is intended to proceed along three major paths:

1. Technical and other planning work. The NADF is working to create cohesion among public service providers on aspects of the X.500 technology not sufficiently developed in the international standards documents.

2. The creation and operation of a pilot directory service involving all the member public service providers.

3. Providing a commercial X.500 public data network service in North America.

The NADF technical work to date has focused on aspects such as defining the structure of a directory information tree (DIT) for North America, deciding how the upper levels of the name space dealing with country and organizations should be assigned and managed, and agreeing on a common set of authentication and access control policies.

A set of technical documents have been published outlining agreements on these topics. The NADF has recently begun work on the second stage of its program—the implementation of a pilot directory service for North America.

## B.8 THE INTERNET ACTIVITY BOARD (IAB) AND THE INTERNET PROTOCOL SUITE

The technical organization responsible for coordinating the development of the Internet suite of protocols is called the Internet Activity Board (IAB). The IAB was responsible for the standardization of RFC 1006, which is commonly used to deploy X.500 over TCP/IP networks. The IAB is composed of senior researchers with an in-depth knowledge and lengthy history with the Internet. In fact, for the most part, the IAB members are the designers and original implementors of the first Internet suite of protocols and services.

In reality, the number of documents produced by the IAB is quite small. Any member of the Internet community can design, document, implement, and test a protocol or service for use within the Internet suite. The IAB requires that protocols be defined and presented in RFCs, or requests for comments. In contrast to the ISO and CCITT specifications, RFCs include the notion of documenting and disseminating protocol and service ideas that may never be adopted. In fact, protocol authors are encouraged to use the RFC mechanism regardless of whether they expect their protocol to become an Internet standard.

The RFC standardization process starts with the protocol categorized as a proposed protocol. The expectation is that several organizations will independently implement and test the proposed protocol. The motivation of the parallel and separate implementation process theoretically results in an improved version of the protocol being designed and developed. When the appropriate level of stability is achieved, an IAB-member sponsor must be found to champion the protocol in the

IAB. A sponsor is identified and the argument moving it to a standard is made. If the IAB arrives at a consensus in favor, the protocol or service becomes a draft Internet standard. A new RFC is published indicating this new status. The Internet community is typically given six months to review, implement, and test the protocol. Unless major objections are raised or serious flaws are uncovered, the IAB declares the protocol or service an official Internet standard.

## B.9 ISODE CONSORTIUM

The ISODE Consortium was recently formed with the goal of promoting and managing the planned evolution of the ISODE code base including Quipu, its X.500-based directory service. The ISODE code has been in the public domain for several years now and has benefited from the research contributions of many universities and organizations around the world. The code base has become more stable, and an increasing number of commercial and research organizations have come to depend on it. However, there is a growing feeling that the informal management of the code base adopted to date will no longer suffice. As a result, the ISODE consortium has been formed to provide a more orderly and stable evolution process for the technology.

The ISODE consortium has taken the ISODE code out of the public domain (although an unsupported version will still be available on-line through the Internet free of charge). The consortium now charges organizations that wish to acquire copies of the code base. Members of the ISODE consortium pay a membership fee based on the revenues of their organization; this gives them access to the ISODE code base.

Member organizations include most of the original organization involved in the development of the ISODE technology, including University College London, SURFNet (Dutch Research Network), SWITCH (Swiss Research Network), University of Michigan, Performance Systems International (PSI), the Corporation for Open Systems (COS), and more.

# GLOSSARY

**A-Associate:** An operation defined by ACSE to initiate an OSI communication connection at the application level.

**Access Point:** A DSA name and address that may be used to establish a communication association.

**ACSE (Association Control Service Element):** A standard developed by ISO/CCITT to enable the establishment and termination of OSI associations by the application entities X.217 and X.227.

**ADMD (Administration Management Domain):** A collection of MHS entities managed by a common public administrative authority.

**Administrative authority:** An entity that has administrative control over all entries stored within a single DSA.

**Alias:** An alternative name for an object.

**API (Application Programming Interface):** Formalized and fully documented interface to a software module or set of modules. An API is usually published and promoted within the computer industry as a standard interface.

**A-Release:** An operation defined by ACSE to terminate an OSI communication connection at the application level.

**ASE (Application Service Element):** An application-layer entity.

**ASN.1 (Abstract Syntax Notation One):** A standard developed by ISO/CCITT to define the syntax of the information exchanged by application level entities, X.208.

**Attribute:** Information of a particular type concerning an object represented by a directory entry.

**Attribute Type:** The component of an attribute that indicates the class of information given by the attribute.

**Attribute Value:** An instance of the class of information indicated by an attribute type.

**Access Units (AU):** Network interface units that allow access to the MHS environment to a generic set of entities that wish to avail themselves of messaging services.

**Bind:** Protocol operation used to set up an association between two application entities.

**BNF (Backus Naur Form):** Notation used to define the ASN.1 syntax.

**CCITTL:** International Telephone and Telecommunications Organization responsible for developing and approving international standards.

**Certificate:** The public key of a user together with some additional information, which is rendered unforgeable by encipherment by the secret key of the certification authority that issued it.

**Certification Authority:** An authority trusted by one or more users to create and assign authentication certificates.

**Certification Path:** An ordered sequence of certificates of objects in the DIT that, together with the public key of the initial object in the path, can be processed to obtain the public key of the final object in the path.

**Chaining:** A mode of DSA-to-DSA interaction, whereby a DSA forwards an operation to another DSA for execution and then relays the outcome back to the original requestor.

**Client:** A computer process responsible for accessing a set of electronic services on behalf of a human user or another application process.

**Context Prefix:** The sequence of RDNs (Relative Distinguished Names) leading from the Root of the DIT to the initial vertex of a naming context. Corresponds to the distinguished name of the initial vertex of the naming context.

**Credentials:** Information used to establish the identity of a user or resource; typically it consists of a name and a public key.

**Cross Reference:** A knowledge reference containing information about another DSA that holds an entry frequently used by this DSA.

**DACD (Directory Access Control Domain):** An area of the DIT governed by a common access control policy.

**DAP (Directory Access Protocol):** The protocol used by a DUA in accessing the directory service.

**DIB (Directory Information Base):** The collection of information held by the directory.

**Digital Signature:** A mechanism to ensure the integrity and authenticity of the originator of a piece of electronic information.

**DIT (Directory Information Tree):** The logical hierarchical structure of directory information.

**Directory Entry:** A part of the DIB that contains information about an object.

**DIS (Draft International Standard):** The draft version of an international standard being developed by ISO.

**Distinguished Name:** The sequence of RDNs leading from the root of the DIT to the object of interest.

**Distribution List (DL):** Group of users or resources which may be addressed, by electronic mail, as a whole.

**DMD (Directory Management Domain):** A collection of directory entries managed by a common administrative authority.

**DP (Draft Proposal):** A draft version proposal of a standard being developed by ISO.

**DSA (Directory Service Agent):** An OSI application process that provides the directory functionality.

**DSP (Directory System Protocol):** The protocol used by a DSA to cooperate with other DSAs in carrying out the directory service.

**DUA (Directory User Agent):** An OSI application process that represents a user in accessing the directory.

**Internal Reference:** A knowledge reference that contains an internal pointer to an entry held in the same DSA.

**IS (International Standard):** An international standard developed by ISO.

**ISO (International Organization for Standardization):** An organization responsible for developing and approving international standards.

**Knowledge:** The information that a DSA holds on how to locate other entries in the directory.

**LAN:** Local Area Network.

**Management Information Base (MIB):** A repository of network management information.

**Master:** A DSA holding the copy of one or more directory entries to which changes may be applied directly, and that will affect all other copies of the information.

**Message Transfer Agent (MTA):** An OSI application process, defined as part of X.400 MHS, that denotes an active component involved in the transfer of electronic mail messages.

**MHS (Message Handling System):** A collection of protocols to support the exchange of electronic mail.

**Multicasting:** A mode of interaction whereby a DSA may forward an operation for execution to multiple other DSAs and relay the result(s) to the originator of the operation.

**Name Resolution:** The process of locating an entry by sequentially matching each RDN in a purported name to a vertex of the DIT.

**Naming and Registration Authority:** An organization responsible for allocating OSI names and addresses.

**Naming Context:** A partial subtree of the DIT that is wholly self-contained within a single DSA. It begins at a vertex and extends downward to leaf entries or references to subordinate naming contexts.

**NSSR (Non-Specific Subordinate Reference):** A knowledge reference containing information about a DSA that holds subordinate entries whose name, or RDN, is not known.

**Object Class:** An identified family of objects that share certain characteristics.

**Octet:** OSI terminology used to denote a byte.

**OPDUs (Operation Protocol Data Units):** Units of information exchanged between application entities using ROS.

**Operational Attribute:** A class of attributes defined for use by the directory service itself in its own operation.

**O/R Address:** Address of the originator or recipient of an X.400 MHS message.

**O/R Name:** Name of the originator or recipient of an X.400 MHS message.

**PDAD (Proposed Draft Addendum):** A draft version of a proposed addendum to an existing international standard developed by ISO.

**PRMD (Public Management Domain):** A collection of MHS entities managed by a common private administrative authority.

**Public Key:** The publicly known key of a user key pair.

**Query:** A request for directory information initiated by a DUA.

**RDN (Relative Distinguished Name):** The name of a vertex of the DIT.

**Referral:** A mode of interaction whereby a DSA that cannot completely perform an operation itself, returns the name of one or more other DSAs that may be better able to complete the operation.

**Root:** The initial vertex of the DIT.

**Root Context:** The naming context that comprises the root of the DIT.

**ROS (Remote Operations Service):** A standard developed by ISO/CCITT to allow a request/response information exchange between application-level entities, X.219/X.229.

**ROSE (Remote Operation Service Element):** The 1988 version of ROS.

**RPC:** Remote Procedure Call

**RSA (Rivest Shamir Algorithm):** A public key-based encryption algorithm.

**RTS (Reliable Transfer Protocol):** The 1984 MHS protocol defined to reliably transfer message handling data over the session layer.

**RTSE (Reliable Transfer Service Element):** The 1988 version of RTS.

**Schema:** The set of rules concerning DIT structure, object class definitions, attribute types, and syntaxes that characterize the DIB.

**Secret Key:** The key of a user key pair known only by that user.

**Sequence:** An ASN.1 term used to denote an ordered collection of objects.

**Service:** A computer process responsible for providing a set of services in a network environment.

**Service Controls:** A set of parameters defined in the DAP and DSP to constrain the behavior of directory operations in a number of ways as requested by the user.

**Set:** An ASN.1 term used to denote an unordered collection of objects.

**Shadow:** An up-to-date copy of one or more directory entries.

**Shadowing:** The process of maintaining an up-to-date copy of a set of DIT entries.

**SMTP (Simple Mail Transport Protocol):** Popular mail protocol used within the Internet and other TCP/IP-based network environments.

**Subordinate Reference:** A knowledge reference containing information about a DSA that holds a subordinate entry.

**Subtree:** A collection of entries that represent a subset of the DIT.

**Superior Reference:** A knowledge reference containing information about a DSA that holds superior entries.

**Top:** The special object class of which every other class is a subclass.

**UA (User Agent):** An OSI application process, defined as part of X.400 MHS, that denotes a user accessing MHS services.

# BIBLIOGRAPHY

---

CCITT, X.200 Open Systems Model: Basic Reference Model.

CCITT, X.208 Open Systems Interconnection: Specification of Abstract Syntax Notation One (ASN.1).

CCITT, X.217 Open Systems Interconnection: Association Control Service Definition.

CCITT, X.227 Open Systems Interconnection: Association Control Protocol Specification.

CCITT, X.219 Remote Operations: Model, Notation and Service Definition.

CCITT, X.229 Remote Operations: Protocol Specification.

Landweber, L., *et al.* Architecture of the CSNET Name Server. *Proceedings of the ACM SIGCOMM '83 Symposium.* Austin, Texas, March 1983, 146–153.

Mockapetris, P. *Domain Names: Concepts and Facilities.* Los Angeles: USC Information Sciences Institute, RFC 882, November 1983.

Mockapetris, P. *Domain Names: Implementation and Specification.* Los Angeles: USC Information Sciences Institute, RFC 883, November 1983.

Needham, R.M. and A.J. Herbert. *The Cambridge Distributed Computing System.* New York: Addison-Wesley, 1982.

Oppen, D.C. and Y.K. Dalal. The Clearinghouse: A decentralized agent for locating named objects in a distributed environment. *ACM Transactions on Office Information Systems* 1 (3): 230–253, July 1983.

Rivest, R.L., A. Shamir, and L. Adleman. A Method for Obtaining Digital Signatures and Public-key Cryptosystems, *Communications of the ACM*, 21, 2 (February 1978), 120–126.

# Index

# About the Radicati Group, Inc.

The Radicati Group is a leading consulting firm specializing in the procurement and deployment of Messaging Systems and Directory Services. The company advises leading Fortune 500 corporations in the development of Requests for Proposals (RFPs), Vendor Evaluations, and product roll-out.

The Radicati Group also works with leading vendors in the development of product strategies, and market and channel strategies as well as competitive industry analysis.

The company specializes in the areas of:

- X.400 message handling systems
- X.500 directory services
- EDI
- PC LAN messaging and directory services
- Groupware and workflow automation
- Wireless e-mail
- E-mail management

The Radicati Group is an international firm with clients throughout the US, Europe, and the Pacific Rim. The company's market research takes a global perspective, providing clients with the valuable information necessary to compete on a worldwide basis.

The Radicati Group publishes *The Messaging Technology Report,* a monthly analysis publication providing in-depth analysis in the design and use of messaging systems, directory services, EDI, authentication and security, workflow automation, and mail-enabled applications. *The Messaging Technology Report* is authored by Dr. Sara Radicati in cooperation with other leading industry experts.

For more information about our services, please write or call:

The Radicati Group, Inc.
625 Emerson St., Suite 210
Palo Alto, CA 94301
Tel: (415) 857-0963
Fax: (415) 857-0719